FINANCIAL FIRST AID

ESSENTIAL TOOLS FOR CONFIDENT, SECURE MONEY MANAGEMENT

ALYSSA DAVIES

STERLING
New York

STERLING
New York

ISBN 978-1-4549-4466-9
ISBN 978-1-4549-4467-6 (e-book)

Distributed in Canada by Sterling Publishing Co., Inc.
c/o Canadian Manda Group, 664 Annette Street
Toronto, Ontario M6S 2C8, Canada
Distributed in the United Kingdom by GMC Distribution Services
Castle Place, 166 High Street, Lewes, East Sussex BN7 1XU, England
Distributed in Australia by NewSouth Books
University of New South Wales, Sydney, NSW 2052, Australia

For information about custom editions, special sales, and premium
and corporate purchases, please contact Sterling Special Sales at
specialsales@sterlingpublishing.com.

Manufactured in the United States of America

2 4 6 8 10 9 7 5 3 1

sterlingpublishing.com

Cover and interior design by Jordan Wannemacher
Cover illustration by Alyssa Davies and ©iStockphoto

*For the one who feels like they don't have
a best friend to talk about their financial
fears with—you've found a safe place here*

YOU CAN BE IN CONTROL OF YOUR MONEY. YOU JUST HAVE TO FIND WHAT WORKS FOR YOU.

CONTENTS

FOREWORD

THE "HUMILITAINMENT" ERA WAS a time in which all you had
to do was find a person who wanted to yell at people and use
that to create a television show concept about pretty much
anything: cooking, singing, and even dealing with personal
finance. People would tune in every week to watch regular
people get berated, called names, and shamed about the
choices they'd made or the situations they found themselves
in. This genre of reality television in the mid-to-late 2000s
was wildly popular. Luckily, those tropes are dying off.

What we crave now are real people, not caricatures, who
take the time to understand and support people. Leaders
are those who can create safe spaces in which everyone benefits from sharing different lived experiences together, as a
collective. Unified. Having each other's backs.

Alyssa Davies is one of those leaders. A real person. A confidante. A friend. If you're reading this, you likely already know her. But I don't just mean you know her in the sense that you've seen her name or face on an Instagram reel. While you may never have had the pleasure of sharing a coffee, meal, or drink with her, you likely feel that you have a deep connection with this person who seems to psychically know what you are thinking about money. And not just the financial worries like "How much money is supposed to go where?" The really deep stuff, like, "How do I tell my partner that I had an emergency that led to carrying $15,000 in credit card debt before we got serious, and now I'm worried it's been too long to bring it up?" Or, "How do I find a way to sleep at night when I'm riddled with anxiety about what would happen if the company I work for decided to make cuts in response to the pandemic because sales have been down for a year?" and "What do I do when I'm in my probation period at a new job and my boss is sending sexual text messages?"

Not only does she provide a collective support group (Mixed Up Money) that lifts up its members, she has practical, actionable blueprints you can put into practice. Like this book, which focuses on financial first aid. They say great minds think alike, and I've always been an advocate of focusing on what can go wrong (as well as thinking about reaching your financial potential). My number-one rule for people is to disaster-proof their lives. But if I could slot a rule before that, it might be encapsulated by this book's core message, which is how to treat the many financial wounds that so many of us have already experienced, or are currently experiencing, before we can get to a position where we can worry less about money. And these wounds can happen even after we've achieved escape velocity with our personal financial situation. Maybe you're earning good money, budgeting a healthy monthly surplus, and investing, and you've got your will and powers of attorney all set up. Then you lose your job. Or a natural disaster strikes your community. Life can change in a heartbeat. No one is infallible.

Alyssa, from MixedUpMoney.com, is the next generation of personal finance experts, even though she keeps referring to *personal finance experts* as some other group of people. I would say she is a rising star, but the truth is her star has risen already. We may just not have noticed because she's been lifting us all up alongside her.

Preet Banerjee
Personal Finance Expert
Author of *Stop Over-Thinking Your Money!*
Host of *Million Dollar Neighbourhood*

FINANCIAL FIRST AID

INTRODUCTION

WHEN YOU'RE A KID, people are always trying to prepare you for potential emergencies. From fire escape plans to carrying Band-Aids in case of an accident—we're ready for nearly any surprise. The only thing missing? Our money.

When you think back to your childhood, something I encourage every person to reflect on is their first money memory. Mine wasn't anything special. In fact, nothing about my childhood was *eternally* memorable. And in many ways, that's a beautiful thing more than it is sad. It means there weren't any traumatic moments that clouded the way I grew as a woman.

Instead, my siblings and I had full bellies, more clothes than we needed, a home that had space for each of us, and "fun" family road trips—although my sister may disagree with that last one. Some people will read these words and think: spoiled, privileged, upper-middle-class. Others will think my upbringing sounds average and similar to theirs. None are wrong.

These days, instead of feeling fortunate for my upbringing and my family's successes, parts of me feel shame. It makes you wonder—how can the ultra-wealthy walk through their days, in their designer shoes, with their glowing skin never having missed a facial, and not feel like they, too, should be ashamed for having too much. But I guess that used to be me.

Growing up with money means never knowing a life without it.

So, for that reason, it can be hard to understand what might happen or, worse, what does happen, to people who struggle financially—particularly if that person ends up being you.

When I was young and naive, I didn't care to learn about others' perspectives or upbringings. I didn't think to accept that not everyone had what I had or received the same opportunities that I did. It took me a while to realize that life wasn't as seamless and effortless for some people as it was for others. To recognize that some people couldn't call their parents for help with an unexpected emergency. To hear that some people would never live their lives without some form of debt circulating in their minds, making them feel endless amounts of stress.

As a teenager, I remember thinking to myself that it was annoying how over-prepared my mom was. Thirty years later, I've become an exaggerated version of her. I'm constantly prepared with several backup plans and even an eighth plan for when the seventh scenario doesn't play out quite as well as it did in my head.

We all know that an emergency can happen at any time and that most of these emergencies will impact our livelihood. Sometimes, I consider my anxiety to be a burden, but, financially, I've found a way to balance those worries, and now I view them as a sign of strength.

Financial emergencies come in many forms. They can be specific, like a natural disaster that damages your home or a lifelong injury that forces you to reduce your work hours and lessens your income. In any sense, they are the things in life that force us into uncomfortable and stressful positions when it comes to money, staying on top of our bills, and living without fear.

For that reason, emergency funds—yes, plural—are the best way to avoid those forced struggles. When I think about what may happen if I lose my job tomorrow, it's no longer a worry because my emergency fund has me covered. Assuming I'll lose the love of my life and be left both emotionally and financially stunned no longer feels like a scenario I can't manage.

I've got financial freedom because my first aid kit for my money hasn't expired like most of the medicine that sits under my sink. It's packed full to the brim with those same Band-Aids and fire escape plans that I needed as a child, only for my adult self. Now I'm ready to face any emergency that hits my wallet where I don't want it.

Considering my upbringing and how easy my life truly was, until I started to educate myself about personal finance, my only view on money was what my parents had taught me. My understanding was that we always had enough for what we needed and that the rest was meant for enjoying the things we loved.

Yes, of course, it paid the bills and kept a roof over our heads, but it wasn't just for essentials. My memories of money are often fun back-to-school shopping trips with my mom, convincing her that I needed those designer jeans or I would risk being the laughingstock of my entire class, and filling our grocery cart to the brim.

The funny thing about childhood and teenage years, though, is that no matter how many times someone tries to confront you about your future and saving money, unless your family has dealt with these issues, it's all lost.

You don't hear "bills," you don't want to learn about "politics," you think that everything that your parents or grandparents tell you happens in an alternate universe that you will never have to experience because time isn't real and you'll be young forever. Until you're not.

Financial surprises aren't quite the same as a surprise party you plan for your best friend. Instead, they are typically unwelcome and come with a side of hardship.

Learning how to navigate the anxieties that come from

financial expectations, like hitting traditional milestones at the right age, is crucial. After all, how else can you face the unknowns that we all inevitably face when it comes to our money? Although it's ideal to have a backup plan for emergencies, having a backup plan for your everyday financial life is even more important.

Only 41 percent of Americans can cover a $1,000 emergency with their savings.[1] As we'll discuss in this book, planning and saving for the unexpected can make these difficult turning points in life a lot more manageable.

Think about your monthly expenses. Would $1,000 cover your most expensive bill? If you lose your job or end up with unexpected medical debt, what are your options? You need to know how to prepare, what to expect, and have that expert advice at your fingertips to help you navigate life's unknowns. Something like, for example, a global pandemic.

I sometimes joke with my husband about the fact that I wish we could connect wires to our brains and print out a full list of our thoughts throughout the day. How many of my thoughts would be anxiety-related nonsense that makes me question whether I'm doing enough to keep myself and my family safe? It would look something like this:

- ▶ Your child is swinging too high on that swing.
- ▶ We need more money.
- ▶ Don't forget to finalize that work project due next week.
- ▶ We need more money.
- ▶ There is a global pandemic.
- ▶ We need more money.

- ▶ Climate change is going to make our lives much more expensive.
- ▶ We need more money.

Half my thoughts typically revolve around my finances. Even if I think they don't, those insecurities and feelings of fear are indirectly or directly impacted by how much money I have on hand, how much I have invested for my future, and what I can do to control the uncontrollable parts of my life. For the most part, it sounds impossible. No one can control the uncontrollable. But the good news is that we can control how we prepare for these situations.

A good example of this is saving money for emergencies. So many of us are naturally good at saving, but we are, unfortunately, bad at saving with purpose. We keep as much of our money in our checking account as possible for a few reasons:

- ▶ It makes us feel like we have a lot more money than we do.
- ▶ We believe that this will be our emergency savings.
- ▶ We don't know where else to put the money.

So, in a sense, we're all trying to have that same feeling of control. The difference is that you actually need to put those dollars to work in the right way, rather than just crossing your fingers and hoping everything will work out okay. And in that regard, I've been there.

Back in the day, my idea of saving was pretty bleak. Not

only did I not have an emergency fund, but I was also consistently spending my "savings." Financially, my understanding of savings was "not spending it" or "not touching it."

There was no purpose behind my savings, which made it much easier to spend without concern. The problem? It left me in an endless cycle of feeling that I needed more, or, should the worst happen, my only option to tackle a bill would be my biggest fear—going into debt.

Money is the most robust tool we have to control how life's obstacles can impact us. Whether you have a lot or a little, it's essential to make the most of your dollars by setting yourself up for success through financial preparedness.

After all, you can't put a bandage on your debt and walk away. Instead, the best thing to do is to create the ultimate first aid kit to control your finances—and, more importantly, your future. To some extent, we can all agree that money is an emotional and intimidating part of life. Thankfully, this book is here to help normalize the ins and outs of finance and how we can use money as one of our most powerful tools.

The beauty of *Financial First Aid* is that you can read through the entire book to learn what you should prepare for, but you can also hop around to find the exact information you need if you're currently navigating one of life's surprises. You can learn from expert advice and real-life examples of how regular people like you and me can brave the storm and come out on the other side (mostly) unscathed.

For some, hearing the words *your financial future* can make you sweat through every layer of clothing until the people in line behind you at the store start to become concerned that you may be dehydrated—and also a little bit weird. If that's you, I hope you know you're safe here. That your financial future isn't doomed or far off or impossible to secure.

Maybe you're here reading this book because you're ready to take the next step with your money. Maybe you're here because you've already taken those steps but you're still feeling anxious. And, honestly, I feel you. You can only do so much with your money before you think, "Have I already hit a wall?"

Trust me—you haven't. If you want to do something to better your financial future right now and can't even imagine waiting until tomorrow, or the next chapter, here are three things you can do immediately to set yourself up for financial success and help eliminate your money worries:

1. Invest your money. Even just $100. It will take you so much further than you might realize.
2. Toss a bonus into your savings account today. Just because. Just $20.
3. And, most important, start to build up your emergency fund. You will not regret it.

Car tires tend to find nails, and phones tend to slip out of our hands into toilets. Human beings are clumsy and adorable (and also extremely expensive). On the other hand, the world is also shifting. It's getting hotter; its expectations are higher; we now know we cannot keep living as though nothing bad will ever happen and that there are no consequences of our actions.

As a society, we are obsessed with consuming more rather than focusing on what we already own. This mindset can make money feel less like a tool and more like something that comes and goes in a much more fluid sense.

These things can be hard to acknowledge because we're doing all of the same things as our peers, or we want all of the same things as everyone else, but the reality is, being normal and doing what our friends and family tell us to do is never going to make us feel less stressed about money. And if I told you that you could do something right now to change that feeling, we both know you'd be willing to at least learn about your options.

Because although owning a home and getting married and having kids and securing that dream job are all things that we grew up thinking were the ultimate goals in life, the real goal and the real win is being able to walk through your days without carrying financial burdens that add to your stress and your inability to sleep soundly or watch a movie without picking up your phone to disassociate.

You can do plenty of small, helpful things to change your financial life. However, don't forget to also take care of the big-picture things you need to do when it comes to your future. For that, you'll have to crack open and read more of this book.

1

YOU NEED AN EMERGENCY FUND (OR THREE)

THE IMPORTANCE OF HAVING SAVINGS TO PROTECT YOUR FINANCIAL FUTURE

HAVE YOU EVER WONDERED why we say, "Learning the hard way"? Most definitions of this saying explain that we are more likely to understand a lesson by experiencing it firsthand. That, or creating a permeability so that you don't make the same mistake twice. But wouldn't life be a lot easier if you could take advice from others to avoid this type of burdened learning?

It's mystifying to me how terrified we are to learn new things. We get embarrassed if we can't do something right the first time because we see others who have been doing this thing—for years, I might add—succeeding.

Parenting has taught me that this embarrassment starts early. My toddler gets perpetually frustrated when she can't do something right on her first try. Whether it be tying her shoe or opening the fridge, if she can't do it correctly on her first

13

attempt, she won't keep trying until she gets it. She'll leave and come back another time, plus or minus a few tantrums.

So, imagine if, from birth, someone constantly reminded you that you don't need to be embarrassed when you're learning. Would we be faced with less shame when navigating new projects or experiencing new things? Likely yes. It's something we're adamant about in our house. You need to teach your kids two lessons:

1. You can and should be proud of yourself. Because validation should come from within before it comes from external sources. For that reason, instead of saying, "I'm so proud of you," we also like to ask the question "Are you proud of yourself?"
2. You should never be embarrassed to learn or fail.

For crying out loud (literally)—it takes us three months to learn how to hold up our own heads and an entire year to learn how to use our legs—why would anything else we attempt to learn be any different?

In my experience, people who can correct bad habits they've had for years are the examples we should be following. Why? Because to correct a bad habit takes serious commitment and control. The same goes for adults who are willing to admit that past thoughts and behaviors are not okay, correct, or appropriate.

Most of us would rather continue to allow that bad habit to stick, because it's been working for us, so why would we bother to change? Is it going to click overnight? Of course not. If I learn I can change my money habits and want to change them, will thinking about it hard enough really work? Well, no. Because before it becomes an unconscious habit, it will take many more times of correction and relearning how to manage my spending.

It takes a ton of effort to continually acknowledge when you say or do the wrong thing because you need to unlearn that behavior as many times as you have learned it. If you have had 10,000 racist thoughts or made 10,000 impulse purchases, you need to do or think about something the right way 10,001 times to truly change that mindset. At least, that's what I believe.

Learning to accept that you were wrong is hard for most people, not because they don't subconsciously agree but because they're too scared or too uncomfortable to learn, regardless of how it impacts themselves and others.

The thing about learning is that it starts and stops with us. We have to expect that what we know is as big as we are—as big as our circle and as big as our experiences.

Learning takes time and learning about money is no different. Humans, for some reason, often take comfort in being average because the status quo is "enough." Unfortunately, when it comes to finance, doing what's average isn't enough. Because most of us average folk are terrible at prioritizing our financial future.

Have you ever looked at someone one way and later realized that your view of them as a person was wrong the whole time? Before I knew anything about personal finance or managing money, I was blind to responsible spending. I wanted to have everything I couldn't afford, and I was willing to take out new credit cards to ensure that happened.

Not anymore. Shortly after money became a focus in our lives, my husband said something that I hadn't ever thought about.

"I look at things so differently now," he said. Intrigued, I asked him what he meant, and he said, "I saw someone drive a nice car up to our condo building and thought to myself, 'Nice car. But can you even afford that?'"

CAN YOU EVEN AFFORD THAT?

What a point-of-view change. Instead of assuming someone is rich based on "stuff" they may or may not have the ability to pay for—what if we *actually* knew what their financial situation was like? Perception is a funny thing. Believing you have the financial means to pay your bills is vastly different from actually having the financial means to pay your bills.

> ▶ According to a 2019 survey, 59 percent of adult respondents in the United States admitted to living paycheck to paycheck.[2]
>
> ▶ In that same survey, 35 percent spent more money than they could afford to in order to participate in experiences with friends.[3]
>
> ▶ And 28 percent of US adults had no emergency savings.[4]

NOW HOW DO YOU FEEL
ABOUT YOUR FINANCIAL SITUATION?

Rather than becoming a statistic or burying these facts in the back of our minds, let's remember them. Let's keep them as a reminder that we need to live within our means, we need to manage our budget, and we need to purchase things we can afford—not things we want to afford. Borrowing money today from your future self is a sure way to avoid retirement. Smart financial decisions you make today can bring a wealth of success in the future. These are the same money rules that we hear from the financial experts over and over. So you may be sick of being told to just "be better" with your money. But they aren't always wrong.

Of course, as a human being, you are going to have bad days, make terrible decisions, and have poor judgment. But, as my good internet friend Amanda Holden, of *Dumpster Dog Blog*, would say, "You did an asshole thing, but you are not an asshole." The difference is that some of us are more fortunate than others when we do those asshole things. We have help. We have a lot of privileges—and this is especially true with personal finance.

I'd be doing all of us a disservice not to note that some of us have to worry more than others when it comes to unexpected expenses. Some of us can easily lean on our parents for support. Others can't even call their parents for a casual conversation.

Some of us have access to better jobs because we've been

able to take advantage of higher education. Others among us have to work much harder to prove ourselves and our skill set. Some of us are white. Some of us are slim. Some of us are male. Some of us are heterosexual. Others are none of those things—and, statistically, that puts them at a disadvantage financially.

Because data always helps us paint a picture, the average net worth per capita among white Americans is around $437,000 per person. In contrast, it's closer to $105,000 among Black people and a staggering $53,000 for Hispanic people.[5] A large part of this comes from generational wealth or the assets we pass from one generation to the next.

Privilege can be subtle in how it is passed from one person to another. It can be through traditional means, like an inheritance, or it can be passed through paid education, help with a down payment, or simply having the ability to ask for help when you're struggling (or in an emergency).

I learned that many people think that privilege is normal. You now know that used to be me. That naivete can turn to shock when you hear that what you learned in life is not what someone else has learned—or that others will never be able to relate to you. But that's the crucial part of learning about other people's experiences.

It's important to acknowledge that some of us have a significant advantage and that these issues continue to contribute to the wealth gap. It's not one person's fault, but it's very typical of people to feel defensive or feel a need to justify their privilege.

For example, saying that your parents worked very hard

to get you something or provide for you can imply that other families don't work hard. The same goes for standing by the fact that you think it's no one else's business where you got your start or how large corporations spend their money. That's fine, but remember to offer that same option to people who receive financial support from the government and where they spend their money.

Opening up a narrow perspective can help us understand and be grateful for what we have, which can be especially important when we start to understand all of the financial emergencies that can happen over a lifetime.

Not every piece of advice is going to work for you. Not everything I say is going to hit you as hard as it might hit someone else. But that doesn't mean you don't need to learn about that thing. If anything, it's equally vital because it shows you the truth behind money and its various impacts on people.

Experts tell us many things, including how much of a down payment is best and whether we should lease or finance a vehicle (both debatable). But what they don't tell us is that there are layers of small decisions behind each significant financial choice we make.

Emergency funds are an excellent example of something that requires layers of decision making. Why? Well, because there is more than one type of emergency—particularly if you have a more complex situation.

I have three emergency funds, and, to some of you, that might seem like overkill. To others, it may not seem like enough.

You might be thinking to yourself,
"Okay, I'll bite, what is an emergency fund?"

An emergency fund is a savings account we keep to protect ourselves financially when something unexpected disrupts our livelihood. Many people feel as though they can't afford to save up money for a financial emergency and that, instead, they'll rely on their credit card or line of credit in a worst-case scenario.

Unfortunately, during the global pandemic of 2020, we learned that crossing our fingers and hoping everything will be okay is not a viable plan. We need emergency funds to keep us on track financially, protect our well-being, and help reduce the stress and anxiety surrounding the unknowns.

When it comes to money, I like to call learning the hard way the "hard way tax." If we forgo protecting ourselves financially, we'll have to pay a variety of taxes—whether it be interest on the debt we're forced to use to pay the bills—or the emotional burden of borrowing from our community of loved ones. The hard way tax is a complex tax to face because it's one that wasn't made by our own choices; rather, it was the product of the unexpected moments that come out of nowhere and set us back several steps from any progress we had made.

The good news here is that you don't actually suck at money. But, unfortunately, so many financial institutions, financial experts, and people want you to believe you are bad at managing money; however, truthfully, you can't be bad at something you haven't even given yourself time and space to experience or learn.

Not to mention, there are plenty of systemic issues at play that make it that much harder to get ahead. For example, when I first began to focus on money and my financial habits, I convinced myself that I was doing so poorly with my budget and couldn't get ahead because I was spending too much on small non-essential purchases.

The reality is, I couldn't get ahead because I had student loans for a university degree and thus finished postsecondary education making only slightly more than minimum wage and struggling to pay my rent. It took nearly five years to stop putting myself down for doing everything I could, like working multiple jobs and avoiding spending money on things I loved. And I had to stop blaming, shaming, and guilt-tripping myself for the things that were outside of my control.

Having an emergency fund can protect you from learning the hard way in many areas of life, including your relationships, your career, as a homeowner, and as a human being who is vulnerable to the many obstacles that life seems to throw our way.

So, what type of emergency funds should you have? At the very least, a general emergency fund that could cover your essential expenses—like housing, food, and utilities—is a necessity. Most experts recommend saving three to six months of these costs in a high-interest savings account.

But, after a global pandemic, multiple uncomfortable work situations, and watching some of my friends fall in and out of love with their partners, it's obvious that what the experts say doesn't always cover *every* situation and shield *every* person from the unexpected.

Three essential emergency funds that I've come to love include ones that:

- ▶ Protect yourself
- ▶ Protect your future
- ▶ Protect your shelter

TO PROTECT YOURSELF, one of my favorite emergency funds is the F*ck Off Fund—a term coined by Paulette Perhach in a 2017 *Billfold* article[6] that went viral. Essentially, this fund can protect you from a multitude of things in life that we shouldn't have to deal with.

Whether it be an abusive relationship or an unsafe workplace, having the ability to walk away without any fear of paying your bills or drowning in the what-ifs is a kind of peace that we all deserve. As Perhach writes, "Whether the system protects you or fails you, you will be able to take care of yourself." Most of the time when I'm talking to an individual person, in or out of a relationship, they all strive to have independence. They all want to be equal to their partner. This type of emergency fund is your ticket to having that security and independence you desire.

TO PROTECT YOUR FUTURE, a general emergency fund to cover things like a flat tire or job loss can eliminate the need to forgo any other financial goals. For most of us, if our pet suddenly gets sick and requires emergency surgery, we have to pull from our savings or, worse yet—pull out our credit cards—to cover the bill.

Instead, an emergency fund can protect your future by allowing you to continue to put your money toward the things you want, rather than the things you need in moments of difficulty. No one wants to have to sacrifice their retirement plans or withdraw from their retirement funds to cover any type of emergency. Your future and your financial freedom rely on this specific fund.

TO PROTECT YOUR SHELTER, as a homeowner or otherwise, you can build a fund to cover the breakdown of your most expensive appliance (or two). This additional fund will keep you from struggling to make ends meet while also tackling another household bill. The roof you put over your head is something you cannot afford to ignore.

Ultimately, it may seem like a lot of work to create three separate emergency funds. But, when you suddenly feel unsafe in your workplace, get rear-ended on your drive home, or have to replace your furnace in the middle of winter, you won't struggle to dig yourself out of a financial deficit that would completely tank the average person.

Is it silly to be a what-if person and let anxiety run rampant in your mind? Obviously. But, if you're anything like me, taking these steps to protect yourself can at least provide some peace of mind and instill a sense of control that we all desire when it comes to handling the unpredictable.

You don't have to learn the hard way. Instead, you can prepare for what's ahead rather than reacting when that time finally arrives. Because at one point or another, all of us face a financial emergency that can make or break our future. What should you be asking yourself when it comes to your emergency fund preparation? Well, the most important person involved in your money is—well, you. So, instead of focusing on what everyone else is spending, what everyone else is earning, and what everyone else is buying, focus on yourself. What do *I* earn? Where do *I* want to spend my money? How can I make the most of *my* financial situation? The only person you can compare yourself to is *you*.

You probably worry that you'll never stop worrying—and, honey, same! A typical money worry is wondering whether or not you'll ever feel financially secure. So here are the questions you need to consider if one of your money worries is whether or not you'll ever have fiscal confidence:

- ▸ How much money saved in *my* bank account would make *me* feel financially secure?
- ▸ What does *my* ideal lifestyle include?
- ▸ Do my income and my spending align with this picture?
- ▸ What does *my* future look like?

No one will think you're selfish for making sure that you are taking your financial future seriously. No one will question how you plan to accomplish this or judge you if you don't happen to hit your goals at the estimated deadline. Why? Because these financial goals are yours and yours alone.

YOU NEED TO LOOK AT EMERGENCIES AS OPPORTUNITIES

Bob Lai, a personal finance blogger, immigrated with his family to Canada from Taiwan in 1995. He was thirteen years old and suddenly growing up in a country with a different language and different rules. "I distinctly remember that my parents couldn't get a credit card when we moved to Canada," says Bob.

For his household, this meant a steep learning curve and a frugal lifestyle. Money was a subject of frequent conversation for Bob and his family; and, for that reason, emergency funds have always been front and center as he raises a family of his own.

After being turned down multiple times for a credit card, his parents finally advocated for themselves by proving their credit history with old bank statements from Taiwan, and proof that they managed their finances responsibly. That was enough for the bank to finally approve their application.

Regardless, though, when you can't easily access credit or the appropriate accounts to achieve financial security, money becomes a much larger conversation.

Most of Bob's relatives—including his own father—retired in their early forties, making his desire to understand money that much more critical. "In terms of preparing things, my entire family came from a farming background," says Bob. "We were always taught to save for rainy days and only to spend what you earn."

Because Bob is used to living frugally and spending as little as possible, he tries to focus on the positives rather than assuming the worst. "Chances are, the worst will happen, but rather than label our extra money an emergency fund, we call it an opportunity fund." In his mind, these are inevitable expenses that we should all be saving for.

But how do you actually save for a general emergency fund?

If you heard me say that three to six months is the ideal emergency fund and then heard me say you need three of these funds, you might be ready to throw in the towel already. Instead, let's look at a logical way to tackle this financial goal—even if you struggle to save in general.

The first thing you should do when creating a financial goal is to determine how much you actually need, based on your lifestyle. It's easy to hear an expert say what you need and think that's the only option. In reality, we all have different expenses and different goals.

So, to get an accurate number, you'll first have to determine your bare-bones budget. To make things less stressful, focus on saving enough to cover one month of expenses first. If it's $2,000 or $6,000, that can seem like a lot of money to save in addition to meeting your other financial obligations. But by breaking it down into a small monthly contribution, you can feel better about your attempt to save for your first emergency fund. Once you hit one month, you can start to tackle two. You can keep building on this goal until you feel financially secure.

Say you need $2,000 for one month of essential expenses. Determine what you can afford to put aside each month by doing the math to see what's left over after each pay period. If you earn $3,000 each month, you would have $1,000 a month to save for your other financial goals, like retirement or a down-payment fund. Since an emergency fund might come in handy sooner than either of those other funds, you might decide to put the bulk of this month's money toward that.

Once you know how much you need, the next step is to find a safe place to save without the temptation to touch this money for non-essential purchases. A high-yield savings account is a perfect place to store your emergency fund because it's easily accessible and low risk.

From there, you can set up automatic transfers each pay cycle to send a certain amount of your income toward your emergency fund. Unfortunately, not every single financial task and savings goal is fun. But what's less fun is having to give up something you were looking forward to because you had to spend your savings for traveling or a new wardrobe on a new car after ol' Betsy, the 1999 Honda Civic you've been driving since high school, finally kicked the bucket.

But, Alyssa, I'm really bad at saving money!

Hey, I get it. They say reaching your first $1,000 in savings is hard. Yes. But what's even more challenging is trying to save your first $10,000. It seems nearly impossible some days. Still, somehow, some way, my net worth went from a $13,000 deficit to over $20,000 in assets within two years.

Honestly, I'm still amazed that I did it. The best part is that I didn't have to reinvent the wheel—I just followed the basic and simple rules of finance. Don't overspend, track your spending, increase your income, live frugally, be responsible—you know, everything your parents tell you that you hate to hear.

Well, speaking from personal experience, it does work. That is, for me. It works for me.

HOW DO *YOU* SAVE YOUR FIRST $10,000?

One option is to think small, not big. Do you think you could afford to save $5 a day for an entire year? I mean, could you set up a daily e-transfer and ignore your savings account as that cost-of-a-latte amount transfers out? Would you even notice it had moved? I know, it sounds silly. So why would anyone set up an automatic payment so small? Well, because at the end of the year, you'll have $1,825 saved without even batting an eye, that's why.

Instead of the added pressure of putting a lump sum amount of $150 into your savings account each payday, decreasing the amount and increasing the frequency could be the key to overcoming your financial struggle.

For example, I found it challenging to put money into my emergency fund, so I set up a $20 e-transfer to send that money away every Saturday night. Why Saturday? Well, that's easy. My girlfriends and I go out or my husband and I grab dinner. So at the end of the day, what's another $20 on top of the money I've already spent? I began to realize I didn't even notice. It wasn't as terrifying as putting $100 into that account when I already had several other payments coming out each paycheck. It was a great relief.

Saving money is hard. But why? Well, I like to call this restraint bias. Defined as "the tendency to overestimate one's ability to show restraint in the face of temptation." So, you see, thinking that we won't spend money just sitting in a bank account because we have successfully done it before doesn't mean we can do it consistently.

I want to tell you that you can, but realistically, maybe you can't. I have hardwired my brain to ignore that money, but sometimes even I take out an extra $100 here and there.

"This biased perception of restraint had important consequences for people's self-control strategies," one journal reported. "Inflated impulse-control beliefs led people to overexpose themselves to temptation, thereby promoting impulsive behavior."[7]

So then, it sounds like our best option is to get rid of those impulse behaviors. The best way to do that? Those automated transfers we already spoke about. We are straight-up cutting the middleman (restraint bias) out of the equation by automating our finances. Even better? Why not start by easing into this change?

By starting small with $5 daily increments, we allow ourselves to adjust to more vigorous financial habits without really having to do too much. If you find that $5 is attainable, then you can bump it up a few dollars every couple of months. See how high you can get by vowing to save money each day. For example, if you make around $130 a day, can you afford to give up $5 or $10 of those dollars? Only you can answer that question.

In addition to knowing how much you can save and what tactic works best, it's important for you to really understand your why. Although you know that you need an emergency fund for more than just "the worst possible thing," you should also get more specific about why these savings actually matter. When attempting to find your why, there are three easy places to look: your goals, dreams, and income.

Goals are essential because, without goals, saving becomes irrelevant. Pooling your cash into an account with no meaning can become draining and provide zero fulfillment long term. Goals can motivate you to budget better, learn more and generally be better informed about your money.

Your dreams are what allow you to be creative with your savings. Knowing what you hope to accomplish in the future, with or for family, and where you plan to live and earn, are some of the best ways to understand why saving for the unexpected is critical.

We need to save no matter what our income level, but saving more when we have less will help us prepare for a future increase in income and, more importantly, it'll enable us to exist on whatever we earn, even if that amount stays stagnant. I know we're all sick of hearing people say the key to success is to "live within your means," but it's been so prevalent because it is genuinely the biggest downfall for young adults trying to find their way. I believe the number-one cause of debt is having reduced income and the same expenses.

I've said it before, and I'll say it again: Finding financial practices that best work with your lifestyle takes a little bit of trial and error. You're going to have to test the waters to see which options are best and how you can adjust them to set yourself up for success.

Emergencies are opportunities to prove to your future self that you can handle each one of life's obstacles with ease, and I'm going to share with you the best tactics and strategies to put yourself in a better spot than you ever thought possible.

Whether you feel one of these emergency funds is more vital than another, to save for yourself, your future, and your shelter are non-negotiable these days. It's just a matter of breaking down which of these funds will come in handy now—or down the line.

TAKEAWAYS FROM THIS CHAPTER:

▶ You can and should have more than one emergency fund, depending on your lifestyle. Three funds I recommend are: to protect yourself, your future, and your shelter.

▶ Experts will say you need three to six months' worth of expenses saved, but that might not be enough for you. Looking at your lifestyle and your needs can help you find a real number.

▶ The best place to save your money is in high-interest savings accounts that you won't be tempted to withdraw from unless necessary, but also that you can access quickly when needed.

▶ Automatic transfers are one of the best and easiest ways to start to build up your emergency funds.

2

HOW TO EVALUATE
YOUR SAFETY NET

GET TO KNOW WHAT OPTIONS EXIST
OUTSIDE OF AN EMERGENCY FUND

IN THE MIDDLE of my first-ever global pandemic experience—and truly, I hope the last pandemic I experience in my lifetime—I turned thirty years old. It was a year of self-discovery, grief, expression, and challenges. My birthday weekend was great, but it wasn't exactly how I had planned to say my final goodbyes to the most selfish decade of my life.

Instead of the initially planned girls' trip to Mexico, I spent most of my time doomscrolling in panic, followed by watching old TV shows to avoid thinking about "What more could possibly go wrong?" scenarios.

At this point in my life, I feel I have learned many lessons about money, and 2020 wasn't willing to slow those lessons down. In some ways, this global pandemic has changed our society for the better, with more energy spent focusing on systemic racism and governments that have never been motivated by our best interests. But in other ways, it has shown our weaknesses and our lack of empathy, and it has put some of my friends and family members in very difficult situations.

Suddenly, after forcing people to talk about money at every event and coffee date I said yes to attending, it wasn't always me who wanted to discuss what we should be doing to prepare for our financial future. People around me were now interested in one of my hobbies, my passions, and my experiences. Because, suddenly, the people around me were facing financial stress and instability for the first time ever.

Let me step outside the topic of money for one second to talk about home security systems. Weird, I know. But I promise it's relevant.

You see, for most homeowners, security systems sound like an amazing idea. Why wouldn't you put up cameras and hire a company to watch over your six-figure asset when you can't be there to do it yourself? Yet, for some reason, most of us will avoid installing a security system or paying for the company support until we've experienced a break-in or robbery.

Most of us walk through life thinking that bad things will never happen to us. And then, COVID-19 broke a window and we had no way to prevent what was to come other than to work backward.

In two years, we were forced to cram in a lifetime of money lessons. Fortunately for me—or unfortunately, depending on how you view things—my last decade is chock-full of financial mistakes I'll never be able to fix. So I feel comfortable discussing the inevitable emergencies we will all face with our money if we don't plan ahead.

So when you think of the unknowns that 2020 and 2021 unveiled in your life and planning ahead in case this same situation rears its head again, something you absolutely need to do is assess your safety net.

STEP 1: CONSIDER HOW MANY SOURCES OF INCOME YOU HAVE

A couple of the biggest realizations that the pandemic brought to light were that having multiple streams of income can protect you at the worst of times and that we, as employees, will always be disposable to a company.

The number-one reason you need multiple streams of income is because your job owes you nothing. At any point, and far from within your control, you can lose your full-time income. It happens daily, and it's not always easy to anticipate.

I never want to have to worry about losing one source of income and not being able to continue to earn a living without it. Instead, I focus heavily on making my money work for me in unique ways and expanding those streams of income to find more financial stability.

WHAT ARE THE MOST COMMON STREAMS OF INCOME?

1. Earned income—money you earn from a full-time job

2. Profit income—money you earn from a side hustle or product

3. Dividend income—money you earn from investing

4. Interest income—money you earn from saving

5. Rental income—money you earn from real estate investments

6. Capital gains—money you earn from the stock market

7. Royalty income—money you make off a piece of work sold to another company.

The benefits of having multiple sources of income are to create that financial security most of us crave, to eliminate the fear of an unsafe work environment, to diversify your investments, to increase your income, and to find passive ways to earn money without adding more to your already-full plate.

You can help yourself create more streams of income by looking at what you already have, discovering the why behind your desire for financial security, and by tackling one thing at a time.

For me, working has always been a massive part of my life. From the moment I got a job at sixteen years old, I fell in love with the feeling that I was receiving a paycheck and having the freedom to choose what I wanted to do with my earned income. I love to work, but not for the typical reasons that most people love work. For example, I work from home, so I don't see any co-workers for the morning and afternoon small talk, and I don't get free cake when it's someone's birthday.

I love work because it gives me options in life. I love work because the more you embrace your different strengths, the more opportunity you have for growth and the more opportunity you gain to increase your earning potential. One of the reasons this is so important to me is because I'm a mom. To ensure a safe and happy and healthy future, you need multiple streams of income. And this goes for everyone—not just parents.

To begin to grow your sources of income, you should first start with a natural source. For instance, if you already have a full-time job, start to explore what type of investing you can do to earn more passive income. If you are already investing in a retirement fund, consider opening a personal investment account to diversify your portfolio further.

The second way to grow your income is to be patient. One of my best sources of income is my side hustle, and that took many years of building a network and work that fit my schedule. For me, the feeling I get every single time I hit a financial goal is reason enough to continue down the path of financial success. Of course, there will be bumps, there will be difficult times, but the more you protect yourself with diversity, the better off you'll be.

STEP 2: LOOK AT YOUR NETWORK

Having the budgetary means to take care of yourself in an emergency situation is wonderful. But for many of us, life and its demands don't always allow us to prepare for a difficult time—even if we do everything right.

For that reason, consider who, if anyone, in your network would be able to provide help without judging you. Help doesn't always have to be financial. If someone is able to help you with caregiving, or another form of service, it's important to recognize the value of community when it comes to unexpected surprises.

In these situations, assess what type of community or public resources you can keep in mind during moments of pure financial chaos. Although an emergency fund is important, resources and people are equally as valuable.

STEP 3: BE OPEN TO ALL OF YOUR OPTIONS

On that note, don't discredit the power of crowdfunding in an emergency situation. Using networks and platforms like GoFundMe is a common resource for anyone struggling to pay their medical bills or support families who have experienced a loss of any kind.

Reading this, many people may think it's inappropriate

for other people to deal with another's debt or financial difficulty. But the reality of the matter is that society is not built for every single one of us to succeed. If you don't worry about money, you have a certain type of privilege that not many others will ever get to experience.

So much of money comes with shame. The feeling that we don't have enough, aren't doing enough, and will never be enough is inflicted on us daily and prevents us from reaching out in moments of distress. The minute we stop letting that feeling of shame stand in our way, the better off we'll be.

According to a report from the National Opinion Research Center at the University of Chicago, although 60 percent of Americans believe that the government should take the majority of the financial responsibility for medical bills, 61 percent of people have donated to a relative's, co-worker's, or acquaintance's campaign, and 35 percent have donated to a complete stranger.[8]

If you know that emergency funds can prevent financially debilitating life challenges and if you take stock of your safety net before those emergencies show up without an invite, you can confidently go through life knowing you've done your best to protect your money and your mental health. Oftentimes, the greatest life lessons about money come from mistakes.

But, for me, taking accountability for my actions has been the best way to understand where I went wrong and what I need to do to avoid those same mistakes in the future. We are human, and we learn by doing. And sometimes, we do the wrong things. The best way to handle those mistakes is by taking the time to digest the ideas you need to implement to do better in the future.

A significant part of my financial fears comes from the unknown and an inability to control what happens in the future. But, because I've learned that we can only do our best with what we can control, preparing for those moments of adversity has proven to be a much better option than pretending I'm invincible.

With money, even if you do everything right, you will still make mistakes along the way. But, thankfully, financial security can save your life—and has saved mine more than once.

HOW CAN I ASK MY FAMILY OR FRIENDS FOR FINANCIAL SUPPORT?

Melanie Lockert, the author of *Dear Debt,* says that the two most essential parts of this situation are (1) to be honest with others and (2) to set expectations with yourself and others.

She says it's crucial to be honest with your loved one about the situation you're in, how it's affecting your life, and why you're asking for help. Don't attach any conditions to your ask, and understand that you may hear a "no." If your loved one agrees to offer financial support, be clear about expectations.

- ▶ Will you pay it back, or is it a gift?
- ▶ If you can pay it back, how long will that take?

It's also essential to evaluate your relationship with the person you're asking.

- ▶ How close are you?
- ▶ What are their financial means?
- ▶ How will asking affect your relationship with them?

For example, you may find it easier to ask a sibling or parent for money than a friend. But, depending on your family life, maybe that is reversed. Loved ones who may be in this position should think of it as a gift.

To avoid shame, understand that asking for help is brave. Of course, there is a risk of judgment from friends or family, but hopefully, your true friends and family can say a hard yes or no with both parties feeling okay about it.

If Melanie were in this situation, here is what she would say:

"Hey, I wanted to talk to you about a sensitive matter. I'm in [X difficult financial situation]. I feel [emotions, feelings], and it's hard to [challenges, struggles]. I'm wondering if you'd be able to help me out in any way. If you are in a position to lend me money, I intend to pay you back $X per month, starting next month."

As a word of caution, remember that accepting money from friends or family can be a tricky situation to navigate. For that reason, if you are fortunate enough to receive financial support from a loved one, be sure to set up an arrangement and discuss what this loan looks like. If you are expected to repay the money to your loved one, be thorough and clear in how long you might take to pay them back, whether they would like you to pay interest, and be sure to ask what their expectations are.

STEP 4: MAKE SMALL CHANGES TO EASE YOUR MIND

Worries are one of my biggest challenges in life. I worry about anything and everything, including things that haven't happened and couldn't happen, and things my mind is sure will occur.

What if that tree falls on my car overnight?

What if I find out I have an incurable disease?

"What if I'll never be able to pay off my debt?

I've always had the what-if mindset growing up. But, you see, I find that it helps me ensure that no matter what happens, I (in some weird way) will have control over the outcome and that if any of those what-ifs actually happen, I'll be ready because I already thought about them.

The truth of the matter is that we all worry. Some of us tend to do it more than others. Some of us worry because of anxiety and stress. Some of us worry to show that we care. It's what I guess you would call normal. Although, I'll be the first to admit that it straight-up sucks.

I believe that most of our financial decisions and behaviors are often rooted in emotion. So anything we can do to help transform our thinking into feeling more at ease is worth the time and dollars saved. This is something I repeatedly tell myself when I'm feeling any worry creep in.

You've saved for this. You have prepared for this.
You are ready.

The first thing I did was search for solutions to those problems. What clicked for me was the realization that it would be complicated to turn my negative mindset into a positive one unless I could control my worries. That's when I found a way to finally stop the stress and start the weekly ritual that has changed my outlook on worrying.

Every Wednesday, I take fifteen minutes, and I start my activity.

STEP 1: Write down my top five to ten worries affecting my mindset—but never more than ten.

STEP 2: Categorize those worries. Are they solvable or unsolvable? Solvable worries are realistic, happening now, and are within your control. Unsolvable problems are the what-ifs that so annoyingly grace our minds for no reason at all.

STEP 3: Choose one solvable worry to resolve.

STEP 4: Write down all the potential ways to solve that worry. Ask a friend or family member if they have any solutions that you might have missed. Even write down the ideas that you know you wouldn't choose. They are still possible resolutions.

STEP 5: Choose the best possible path that can help you to solve your worry.

STEP 6: Put this plan into action.

In just six steps and fifteen minutes, I give myself some relief from my worries. I'll admit, when I first started this activity, I took time every second day to go over my fears. They were that bad. Now I'm down to once a week and starting to feel I have control over the amount of worrying I do.

Thankfully, there are plenty of resources available out there for these types of concerns—it's just the difficulty of actually finding them. Of course, nothing in life comes without a little bit of thought and practical fear, but the ability to control the amount of worrying is what really matters.

Are you worried about your money situation? Write it down. Worried that you're never going to stop worrying? There are options. Worried that you have a zit everyone will notice? It still counts.

No matter what you have going on (big or small), nothing is less important. Your worries matter.

The second thing I did was embrace my fears as a curiosity. I wanted to learn what types of emergency funds I needed and how they could significantly affect my financial success.

One thing that kept coming up during my weekly exercise

was that I constantly felt on edge because I had this sinking feeling that I didn't have enough of a cushion in my savings account.

It's a common pain point for many people. Balancing overspending is one thing, but over-saving or under-saving issues can be much harder to adjust. So either we run our general checking and savings accounts close to zero, or we keep an excess of funds in our accounts in an attempt to feel secure. Of course, neither of these options is wrong, but finding a happy medium is ideal.

STEP 5: START BUILDING A SMALLER EMERGENCY FUND TO GIVE YOURSELF RELIEF

To find that balance, I convinced myself that a magic number would be the key to solving all of my worries—and, honestly, I wasn't far off. You see, your magic number is that mysterious dollar amount that keeps your savings account from turning into an "I went over budget on my entertainment spending—again" account, over and over *and over* again.

If you're anything like me, you want to find a magic number that allows you to breathe without feeling like a giant horse is sitting on your chest.

For the most part, saving for emergencies can be, well, boring. So I don't label any of my emergency savings accounts as "emergency savings." Instead I label them as "Money to protect your other money. Oh, and also your reckless behavior."

And, yes, you'd better believe that name fits on my online account, where the bankers are now thinking, "Why did we ever let our clients name their accounts?"

You see, even though I had done my part to save three months of my salary after repaying my debt, it never felt like enough. It wasn't enough to allow me to feel comfortable dropping an extra $100 of my regular budgeted income at the grocery store, so how could it be enough to sustain me if I experienced job loss?

I kept thinking to myself, "Maybe once I hit the four-month mark, the five-month mark, or the six-month mark, I'll start to feel a little bit more comfortable. But what about right now? What can I do right now to help myself feel comfortable right this second?"

That's easy. Use the magic number!

I save a smaller amount each month as a rainy-day fund or a financial oopsy-daisy in a separate account. To find my magic number to fill my account, I took my average spend each month and divided that number by six months. So, for example, if your average monthly spend is $3,000, you would put $500 per month into your rainy-day fund.

The best part about the magic number? It's a small milestone you can hit before you have to dive into the world of "Hey, here is six months of my hard-earned money just sitting in an account waiting for the absolute worst to happen."

That silly, small number was all it took to make me feel comfortable—and that was the first time I *really* understood that most of my financial insecurities revolved around the fear of never having enough.

WHAT IF IT'S NOT YOU WHO'S STRUGGLING RIGHT NOW?

If you are in a situation where you're the one wondering what you can do and how you can help someone in a tough financial spot, it's important to remember that sometimes, just being there for them is the best thing to do.

I've asked myself repeatedly: How can you say the right things when everything feels wrong? The pandemic made me feel that it was impossible to help so many people who were struggling. But I tried a few things instead of groveling.

LISTEN TO PEOPLE WHO ARE IN A DIFFERENT BOAT

If someone is having a hard time, and you cannot relate, I'm not sure there are any right things to say. Instead, try to listen. Although it may feel as if someone is attacking you for your blog post or Instagram caption, *sometimes* that person is trying to help you learn. The only problem is that some people are upset with you for reasons that aren't entirely accurate. That's okay, too. You cannot be the go-to person for everyone.

BE A SILENT SUPPORTER

You can help and support people struggling without using any words. For example, if you have friends or family close to you, drop off some flowers anonymously, send them dinner one night, or deliver a handwritten letter acknowledging their struggle. You don't have to speak about all of the ways you can empathize with someone who is having a hard time, because most of the time, it doesn't seem to be as genuine as you may feel.

ONLY SPEAK TO WHAT YOU KNOW RIGHT NOW

As a writer on the internet, I quickly learned not to speak to experiences I haven't experienced myself. It's lovely for you to acknowledge your hardship if you've experienced struggle. We all have. But maybe now is not the time. Saying that you know what it's like to experience job loss and financial hardship is relatable, sure.

But—because, yes, there is a *but*—you do not get to speak to your difficulty as though it equals out to someone else's. So rather than talk about what you think people want to hear, maybe you should write about what you're currently experiencing.

WE ALL NEED TO BE MINDFUL OF OUR LANGUAGE

At some point in their lifetime, every single person has said something mindlessly without thinking about the potential impact they may have on another person. Even if you dance around the subject or try your absolute best to be a thoughtful person, you won't please everyone. One word can be enough for someone to twist what you say into another story. So, instead of feeling that you have nothing good to say or that you're always in the wrong, remember that you are doing your best.

There is nothing wrong with telling people to be proactive with their money or adjust their budgets in a tough time. Problems can arise with *how* you say those words and *when* you give this advice.

If you messed up, apologize. If you've upset one person but made ten other people smile—maybe you did everything right. It's up to you whether you say anything during a difficult time. The bottom line is this: Whatever you say should be practical.

TAKEAWAYS FROM THIS CHAPTER:

▶ You should be aware of how many streams of income you have and see how you can expand this number.

▶ Take stock of your network, and don't be afraid to ask for help in an emergency.

▶ If friends and family aren't an option, you can look at donation and funding platforms to give yourself a fighting chance.

▶ Make small changes in your life to avoid the existential dread and the feeling that you don't have a plan.

▶ Start with a smaller savings goal first to prove to yourself that you can save money for emergencies.

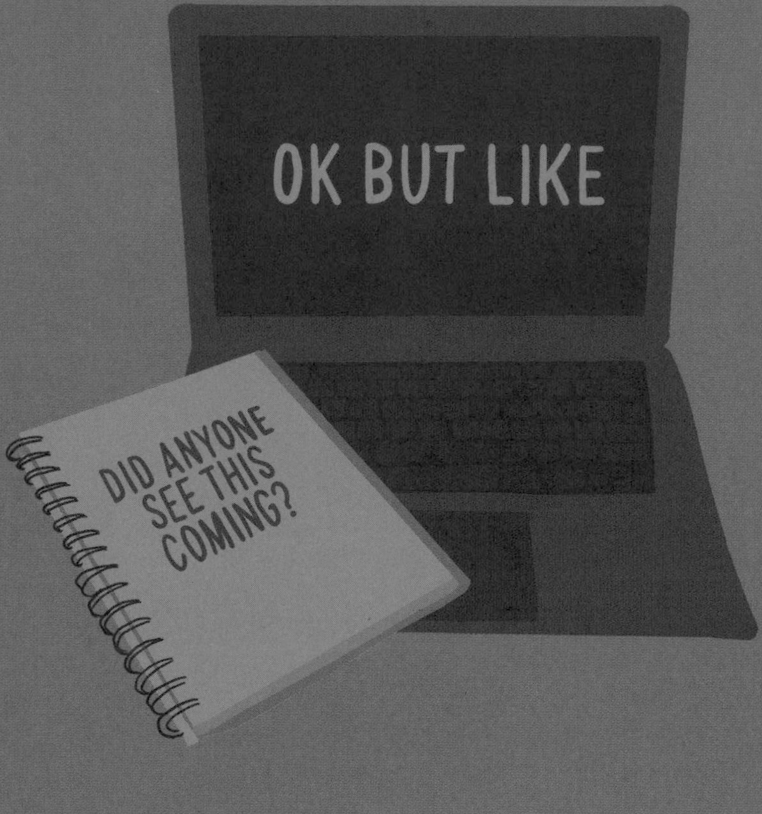
OK BUT LIKE
DID ANYONE SEE THIS COMING?

3

THE WORST HAS HAPPENED. NOW WHAT?

HOW TO ACTUALLY HANDLE FINANCIAL EMERGENCIES

WE SPEND A SIGNIFICANT CHUNK of our youth in classrooms. We learned a lot of stuff in those twelve years, like history, grammar, long division, even how to pour chemical solutions into a beaker. And, hey, some of it I even remember. But if there is one thing missing from my childhood education, it's this: **MONEY.**

We all know this, though. Yet, we don't acknowledge it. We say that we gained most of our money-management experience from parents, relatives, or real-life experiences. But shouldn't it be coming from somewhere else? I mean, isn't education more valuable when we're learning something practical?

Things like if I want to buy a home by age twenty-five,

what do I have to do? What skills do the most in-demand careers require? How will my current classes put me on a path to getting an in-demand job? And, of course, if I pursue postsecondary education, will the resulting job allow me to pay off my student debt within ten years?

Because about one day after leaving my high school graduation, these decisions were all mine. And so was that credit card with a $5,000 limit, student loan debt I didn't necessarily need, and the "What are your salary expectations?" box to fill in on my online résumé. It was terrifying, and my first thought wasn't "Oh man, I'm so thankful they taught me this in class last month." It was more like "Wait, what is a salary expectation?"

No interviewer was asking me to "quickly solve this unsolvable math problem," and no hiring manager was expecting me to know facts about World War II. All they wanted to know was where I'd be living, how I'd be getting to work, and where I saw myself in five years. And none of that had been addressed in my textbooks. So, many financial emergencies were brewing. And they hit me like a ton of bricks. The same might happen to you.

I'm not saying all of these things to give you an excuse or an out. But I am bringing them up to help you realize that the shame you're feeling for being in a challenging financial position isn't always warranted. Sure, sometimes we make bad choices and don't have a backup plan. But politicians do that all the time, and guess what? People still re-elect them. So, what I'm trying to say is that if you're currently looking for a solution to your financial problem, that's all we're going to talk about. I won't blame you for winding up in this spot in the first place—there are enough financial experts out there who already have that space covered.

Instead, let's get inside our own heads and imagine what our worst-case scenarios could be when it comes to money. Because, the thing is, every single one of us might say something different. I want you to ask yourself the following questions:

▶ What aspect of my financial life is overwhelming me most right now?

▶ Why does this part of my financial life scare me?

▶ Are there steps I can take to take control of this part of my financial life?

In my mind, having to deal with any financial difficulties like what I dealt with in my early twenties, is something I never want to deal with again. So, when I start thinking about my future and having two children to take care of for the next twenty or so years, I quickly get flustered and overwhelmed. I tell myself that the worst can (and probably will) happen—*unless* you have a plan.

But because planning isn't always front-of-mind for many of us, it's equally important to understand your options and how to manage those scenarios while living through them unexpectedly. Whether you've experienced job loss, a divorce, an unplanned pregnancy, or a natural disaster—all of which are things we discuss throughout this book—some of the initial steps you take to manage your financial situation and overall mental well-being are universal.

THINGS LIKE ACKNOWLEDGING HOW YOU FEEL ...

Emotions have always been difficult for me. In the first therapy session I ever had, the psychologist told me that I was really good at feeling anger—but that the rest of my emotions could use some work. It seemed funny to me at the time.

Honestly, I thought I was super tough, handled my emotions well, and was calculated in each conversation I had. Nothing I did or said was based on how I was feeling, and I certainly chose to keep it that way with almost everyone in my life.

"Yes, I do get a little bit passionate about minor inconveniences, but don't we all?" I thought to myself. But upon further reflection, I realized that I was struggling to feel excitement, happiness, and sadness when I should.

At twenty-seven years old, I had, according to my therapist, what sounded like anxiety, which turned into depression. Who knew? After years of bottling up my feelings, dodging stress, and avoiding tough conversations with myself, I broke down. I started to feel uncomfortable in situations I would typically throw myself into. I began to be unable to handle any confrontation—which used to be my bread and butter—and I was extremely unhappy with parts of my life that once were my happiest parts. It made me question everything.

I had always assumed that if I save what I need, spend what I should, and work the right amount, everything else would work out. My goals would fall into place, my career would keep me satisfied, and my surroundings would be, well, enough. But, of course, money isn't that straight-forward. And it can certainly inspire a lot of emotions. So I've learned that you need to get to know your relationship with your finances before you can *really* start to make significant progress.

As soon as I hit my thirties, I began to lean in instead of fighting the bad days and hard times. I realized that the more I was willing to accept the difficulties, the more quickly I could rebound, the less time I would spend in the past, and the more time I would have to develop real solutions that made sense.

OR DOING WHAT YOU NEED TO DO, BUT ONLY DOING ONE THING AT A TIME

It can be easy to become unhinged in emergencies. There are so many things on your checklist, but only one of you. For instance, if you find out that you were supposed to go to a birthday party tonight but the date is wrong on your calendar, the to-do's before the event that's now suddenly three hours rather than three weeks away can be overwhelming.

You have to get ready, pick up a present, buy a gift bag and card, and coordinate travel, all while making it seem like there is no way in hell you forgot it was your friend's birthday party because you are so in control of your life it is ridiculous.

But you and I both know you can't do more than one of these things at a time. There is only one of you. So consider making a list of priorities. Asking yourself what is most important in any situation is critical, but this is the most essential step, whether you've made a social-calendar mistake or you're in a financial emergency. Prioritizing the things that matter can help you control how much is on your plate at once.

FOUR WAYS TO MANAGE A FINANCIAL EMERGENCY

1. RE-CREATE YOUR BUDGET

First, you'll need to determine your income and calculate your monthly expenses. Second, find the difference between your income and expenses. If the difference is negative, look at your fixed expenses first to determine what you can reduce in cost or cut back on completely. Finally, look at your non-essential expenses and prioritize them in a list. Try to keep what you can so that you don't feel completely trapped in your budget. But, be realistic.

2. ASK FRIENDS AND FAMILY FOR HELP

We already spoke about looking to your network for help in the previous chapter. Now is the time to reach out and see who and what resources are available to get you through the emergency at hand before you start to rebuild. This will help you avoid getting stuck in this same situation in the future.

3. CALL YOUR PROVIDER OR LENDER

If the worst has happened and you need to call a customer service agent to negotiate a bill, remind yourself that you are not the only person making this call today. Second, do your best to be persistent. When asking for help, you need to accept that it may take more than one phone call or more than one customer service representative to make a change. Regardless, be polite and stay kind. The person you are talking to does not make the rules, and, at the end of the day, the worst thing you can hear is no.

4. LOOK AT COMMUNITY OR GOVERNMENT RESOURCES

In times of financial instability, one of your best options is to consider what your community or local government has in place. Whatever options exist, from a food pantry to a women's shelter, you do not need to feel that you are undeserving of this form of help. In addition, for medical emergencies, food emergencies, or shelter emergencies, there are usually many not-for-profit organizations that are willing to help or point you in the right direction for what resources are available.

5. IF YOU HAVE TO USE DEBT, LOOK FOR LOW-INTEREST OPTIONS

In some situations, debt isn't the worst option we have. Not everyone has family or friends to reach out to, and not all of us can quickly change our budget and recover. However, when it comes to debt, the best way to approach this choice is to make sure you have a plan first. Two good options for low-interest debt are a line of credit (LOC) or a home equity line of credit (HELOC). You can pay both of these debt types back over time and for an interest rate somewhere between 5 percent and 7 percent. If this is your best choice, make sure you work the monthly payments into your new budget to ensure that the numbers line up. If you are unsure, reach out to a not-for-profit debt organization to ask for help setting up a repayment plan.

MOST IMPORTANT, THE KEY IS TO REMEMBER NOT TO PANIC

It can be hard not to overreact when things don't go our way or as we plan. But rather than panicking and letting our emotions take control, the best thing we can do in moments of difficulty is to take some time to think about the best way to manage this misstep.

There are always options when it comes to financial emergencies. So avoid the following things unless you've exhausted all of your other options:

THREE THINGS TO AVOID
IN A FINANCIAL EMERGENCY:

1. USING PREDATORY OR ONLINE LOAN COMPANIES

Avoiding payday loans or loans that come fast and easy is critical when you are in a difficult spot with your finances. Although it may seem helpful at first, the reality of the matter is that these loans can put you into another financial emergency entirely. This type of debt is unsecured, meaning that there is no collateral required. This means you put a lot more at risk. In addition, most of these loan companies are not regulated by the federal government, indicating that their interest rates can be very high.

2. DIGGING INTO YOUR RETIREMENT SAVINGS

It may be tempting to reach into savings when you have nothing else to use to repay your debts. But this should be the last option, rather than one of the top choices for a financial emergency. Most retirement accounts are called retirement accounts because you cannot take the money out until the typical retirement age of sixty-five. For that reason if you withdraw the funds before that time, you will be hit with many fees. This can cause you to lose most (or all) of the earnings you've acquired. But, keep in mind that many plans allow you to borrow against your retirement funds.

From there, you pay the money back through a payroll deduction. This way, you pay a much lower interest rate than the bank would charge, but the interest is going back into your retirement account instead of toward a financial institution.

3. RELYING TOO HEAVILY ON YOUR CREDIT CARD

Revolving debt, such as a credit card, is usually the first thing we consider to bail us out when we're low on funds. It's in our wallet, easy to grab, and no one would know whether you're using it for a casual expense or as a method of survival. As you know, a credit card has a credit limit, and the consumer is free to spend any amount below the limit until you reach your limit. But, remember, this type of debt comes with a higher interest rate of around 19 percent, and that can often become unmanageable if you take on too much debt or use a cash advance. A cash advance is taking money out of your credit card the same as using a debit card—but with additional interest. If you max out your credit card, it's easy to fall into a cycle of only being able to afford the minimum payment each month (which is another financial emergency in itself). Lastly, when you are trying to manage a challenging money situation and start to make a plan, it's always helpful to build small habits that can change your mindset. The reason this can make a difference is that if we don't do our best to acknowledge our feelings, we can become consumed with our money—or lack thereof.

For example, every morning, I pull out my little black journal, and I jot down three things that bring me gratitude. It's simple, practical, and it's changed my outlook on life. This small activity has made me more financially sure about what I want and what I need to do to achieve those things.

In life, I've constantly been battling between old habits—desires to spend all that I earn—and new patterns to save every dollar I earn. As a result, the balance in both my personal life, professional life, and financial life has become one hefty dose of "Everything is fine." Which, as I'm sure you know, never ends up working out.

Many of us have a twisted and confused sense of our relationship with money. We cannot decide whether we need it, want it, hate it, love it, or know why it affects us every single day of our lives. So acknowledging every dollar I receive, spend, and gift to others has given me a sense of gratitude I never thought possible.

Although I haven't hit my financial goals by deadlines, I've still made progress. Although I've dealt with debt and financial struggle, I wouldn't be as money-conscious if it weren't for that experience.

I am grateful to have a job that provides me with food in my belly and a roof over my head. I am thankful to be able to be paid for something I am so passionate about.

In moments of weakness or adversity, it can be hard not to feel embarrassed. But the thing about money is that no matter how savvy or organized we are, not even the wealthiest people can avoid financial mishaps or tough times.

The reality is that most of us are pushing ourselves to our financial limits every single day. The St. Louis Federal

Reserve tracks the nation's household debt payments as a percentage of household income. In 2020, the average debt-to-income ratio was 9.3 percent, which means that the average American spends over 9 percent of their monthly income repaying their debt.[9]

If you account for all of your other monthly expenses, that number implies that we're all just one flat tire or one missed payment away from needing to adjust our lifestyle.

ONE ENCOUNTER THAT HELPED ME REALIZE WE CAN'T CONTROL EVERYTHING

It was a typical Saturday afternoon. Well, normal as in the weather was okay, and I was my "normal" self. Otherwise, it was pretty unique. I was leaving Dallas, Texas, after a financial conference to catch my evening flight back home to Calgary.

After looking at the hotel sign that said a sedan could take me to the airport for $70, I scoffed and immediately opened my Uber app. I got a notification that Barbara was three minutes away in her Chevrolet Malibu. She had a 4.95-star rating, so I was expecting this ride to be everything and more. And by everything and more, I merely mean "safe."

When she pulled up and popped the trunk lid for me, I threw my suitcase in and headed for the front seat. Her purse was sitting there, and I realized that I was the socially awkward Canadian who felt like it was necessary to sit in the front seat so that Barbara didn't feel like a chauffeur. She quickly moved it, and I apologized.

"Sorry, is this okay? I can totally sit in the back seat, too,"

I say in the mousiest voice ever. Barbara is super sweet and tells me to sit there, asks where I'm from, and the small talk (that I usually despise) begins.

When she finds out I'm from Canada, she's curious to know why I'm in Dallas, Texas. I tell her I was at a financial conference for people who love money and write about it regularly. She's immediately intrigued. Either that or confused. Whichever the reason, she continues asking questions.

I tell her that I have a blog where I write about money and that I started it because I had a lot of debt. I explain that I'm now debt free and encourage others to try to do the same. That's when it happens.

"You were meant to get in this car for a reason," says Barbara. "Just this morning, I had a conversation with myself about how I need to get my money in order."

I laugh, and she starts to get animated, telling me about her financial background. But, of course, I'm way too excited and am hoping this car ride isn't over for a while. I want to hear more about this woman who thought me being in her Uber was a "sign."

Barbara tells me all about her love for shopping, buying lunches, and a divorce that damaged her financial plans. The craziest part about all of it? Anytime I said, "I'm so sorry you have to go through that" or "That sucks so much," Barbara immediately cut me off and said: "It's hard, but I'm doing great, and it could always be worse."

It was inspiring to say the least. Not only did I learn that Barbara was a badass babe with confidence to boot, I learned some other precious life and money lessons in that twenty-five-minute car ride.

Not everyone has access to
the financial support I do

In this Uber ride, Barbara and I managed to touch on every financial topic you could think of—including healthcare. When I explained that I could go to my family doctor or the hospital for free, she was blown away. "So, it's free for everyone?" she asked, confused.

I explained that primary healthcare was—but I had to pay a small amount into my work's health insurance plan to get further coverage. Then I explained that at my new job I wouldn't even have to do that. I sometimes forget that it's not like that for everyone. It saddens my heart and hurts my soul, but I'm certainly grateful for what I have. This car ride was a reminder of that. To be grateful is important.

Not everyone gets through life without
significant challenges

Barbara and I talked about how sometimes relationships can be the downfall of our personal finance. She spoke to friends whose families had fallen apart due to one person's gambling addiction, how divorce can genuinely ruin your success, and how sometimes these things happen and you have no control over anything but are still forced to clean up the mess.

We preach about how important it is to have an emergency fund and some fallback plan in case of those unexpected downfalls. Money is not always within our control. There are times we have it, and there are times we don't. It is so important that during the times that we do have it, we try everything in our power to make the best of those nickels and dimes.

The last part of our conversation happened just as we pulled into the airport and is by far my favorite lesson Barbara had taught me thus far.

Barbara told me that her financial inspiration had always been her mother. She said that her mother always knew how to save, take care of family, and make each dollar count. When she reached out to her mom for advice about how to start saving money and pay off her debt, her mom told her, "I started with a quarter."

She was laughing hysterically about how both silly and sad it sounded to start with twenty-five cents in your savings. But she also realized the meaning behind what her mother was encouraging her to do. We all have to start somewhere, and somewhere is better than nowhere.

I was meant to get into Barbara's car that day

One stranger was the reminder I needed that everyone has a different backstory financially. Some of us get head starts, while others have to struggle even to get a start at all.

As much as money is the center of our universe, it encompasses many factors that are sadly out of our control. So thank you, Barbara, and if you ever find this story, I hope you're in the place you want to be. I know you'll be looking directly at the bright side even if you aren't.

Hitting my personal and financial goals doesn't seem as

unachievable once I provide myself with tools and strategies that align with who I am and what I need to stay healthy and happy.

Giving ourselves the freedom to recognize what stress feels like in our bodies and then choosing not to avoid it is what gratitude embodies. Deciding to take money away from one goal and put it toward another can provide happiness, support for your mental clarity, and gratitude.

Money is a large part of who we are as a society and what we need to survive. But we will never survive if we don't lead ourselves down the right path. You are the only person who can take steps to set yourself up for success or navigate a difficult financial situation that's already happening in your life. But, remember, you can only tackle one step at a time.

If the worst has already happened, there is nothing you can do to change that fact, other than allow yourself the time to get back to where you need to be to progress in your financial life. But, unfortunately, unlike most things we accomplish in life, repaying debts or achieving a financial goal doesn't come with balloons, an exciting gift, or a day lounging at the beach. Instead, it comes with the massive relief of stress that weighs on us each day—something only we can feel.

Give yourself the time and give yourself the celebration you deserve for getting through a challenging financial situation. It's not easy, but it can be easier if you put in the financial work to get through it.

TAKEAWAYS FROM THIS CHAPTER:

▸ Acknowledging that your emotions play a large part in financial emergencies is a great way to get out of your head and start to make a plan.

▸ You can do only one thing at a time. First, you should look at your money situation, then explore your options, and, finally, decide which option for financial support is best for you.

▸ Stop beating yourself up for needing help. You aren't less than because you cannot bail yourself out of a sticky situation.

4

PINK SLIPS, LAYOFFS, AND CAREER CHANGES

PROTECTING YOURSELF FROM JOB LOSS AND OTHER WORKPLACE ISSUES

GROWING UP, MY LOVED ONES repeatedly told me that having a fulfilling career was the key to a successful life. So, like many, I did what I was told. I went to school, got an education, found a nine-to-five job, and grinded through repetitive workdays only to realize that one job is never enough in today's economy.

I grew up listening to my parents and grandparents tell stories of working at the same company for twenty to forty years and how important loyalty is—only to realize that, for the majority of us, our employers see us as disposable (and expensive). At any moment, your company could decide that your department isn't serving them in the ways that they anticipated, and, before you know it, you could be out of a job.

This toxic culture puts us in sticky situations when it comes to being one in a pool of millions who are willing to work for less just to get by.

After 2020, imagining job loss might not be very hard for the majority of us. Just three months into the pandemic, my husband was temporarily laid off. We had only moved into our house one year earlier, so we managed our finances on one income—mine—for the first time. It felt stressful, yet we had done everything we were supposed to do to prepare for a situation like this. So instead of panicking, we sat down and went over every detail of our budget. We determined where we could cut back if we needed to and whether it would be best for my husband to look for a new job in a challenging economy or wait for his current position to come back.

After two months of being unemployed, it became clear that his layoff might not be as temporary as we once thought. For that reason, he went for a career change, and after just four months, living on one income came to an end. As a couple who knew the importance of an emergency fund, we had saved up six months of cash, but for others, six months would never be enough.

Over 76 million Americans lost work between March 21, 2020, and January 23, 2021. In addition, some 24 million adults said their households had not had enough food between January 20 and February 1, 2021.[10]

COVID-19 left many out of work and struggling to make ends meet for two years. Stefanie O'Connell, an author and journalist who focuses on money and career, knew this feeling all too well.

With a husband who works on Broadway in New York City, Stefanie knew he'd be the first to lose his job. But she didn't realize that it would be over a year with no end in sight. Nor did she know that she would take a hit as well, with her workload cut in half.

At first, the fear was mild because the couple had saved enough to cover these types of financial emergencies—but their safety net didn't resolve every issue that accompanies job loss. It was an emotionally exhausting experience that came with bouts of depression and feeling hopeless. But Stefanie and her husband kept pushing through, just as we all attempt to do when things get tough.

The pandemic was a stark reminder that even financial experts can struggle, feel pressure, and still not have every answer with all the financial literacy in the world. But the bright side in these moments is that we can rely on them to share what they've learned to help us navigate these experiences when it happens to us. Stefanie shares the steps that helped her family stay afloat:

TOP FOUR STEPS TO TAKE
AFTER JOB LOSS

1. Review your most recent financial history, going back three to six months, to determine how much money you need to cover expenses.

2. Research what resources are available for you in times of crisis, such as at federal, state, and municipal levels; within your personal network; and in your industry.

3. Speak to your lenders to see what options they have in place if you struggle to make payments for a prolonged period.

4. Come up with an anchor that is your baseline essential-spending number. The anchor that Stefanie speaks about was her North Star for survival. Once she had that number, it became easier to conceptualize her financial situation. That way, although the timeline kept moving and there was so much uncertainty, she had a way to ground herself to this one thing that she did know, which served as an anchor and helped her plan around the unpredictable.

As time went on, that anchor helped Stefanie understand how much more they might need to shave from their budget and what financial resources to consider. So to save money, they moved out of the city and cut most of their fixed expenses.

"We talk about the pandemic like it's a once-in-a-lifetime thing," says Stefanie. "But it seems increasingly likely that the need to be prepared for these types of major disruptions is more important than ever."

Sometimes we don't know how long it will take to recover from financial emergencies. For that reason, finding a simple way to protect yourself, whether it be one magic number or one fund, can change your mindset completely.

Focusing on what others do in these moments of uncertainty is the easy part. The hard part is admitting that this could be (or is) you. Consider what you would do if you lost your job tomorrow. Do you know how to prepare for job loss and the ways you can protect yourself financially? What about how to manage life after a job loss? Those moments of transition help us rethink how we approach emergency funds and provide us with a clearer picture of what we might need to feel comfortable.

It's an enormous burden to put these types of pressures on one savings account that can replace a salary. So instead, there are other things we can do to provide a sense of security without feeling like we'll never achieve a number that makes us feel comfortable to move through life without worry.

What are my options?

One thing that I've done to curb the stress of these intrusive—yet inevitable—fears is to understand the power in options. I try to explain to many people in my life the importance of multiple streams of income.

Having multiple income streams means that you have more than one way to earn money, sometimes passive, that doesn't require working several jobs. The most common options are active or passive streams, earned income, profit income, interest income, real estate income, and capital gains income. Although some of these words may mean nothing to you, you likely have more than you realize.

Losing one source of income doesn't have to be the end of your earnings. Instead, you can have a secondary source of income that will step in to save the day. For myself, having a side hustle is an additional stream of income that has protected me in moments of financial distress.

Alongside this, there are other essential considerations if you've recently experienced job loss, such as taking advantage of the offered work compensation, or severance pay. That package has significant monetary value. In addition, use the benefits you may have had as an employee before they expire. Order new prescriptions and set up last-minute healthcare appointments.

Much as you negotiate your salary during performance reviews or upon hire, you are free to negotiate a severance package. If you don't ask, you'll never know—and the worst that can happen, particularly in this situation, is that your employer will say no. Some common things you can negotiate are the amount of pay. For instance, if your company offers a week's salary for every year served, don't be afraid to ask for an additional week or two, depending on the situation. You do not need to sign the package until you are ready. If you need to speak with a legal professional for guidance, this is also an option.

Advocate for yourself and the work you did while you were at the organization. You are the only one who knows how invaluable you are as an employee—and in these situations, it's up to you to prove your point.

PUSHING THROUGH THE WHAT-IFS

Another thing that can feel overwhelming after we lose our primary source of income is the fear that we'll fall behind in saving for significant life events, like a home or our retirement. In life, there will always be periods of setbacks. Focus on your essentials first.

One year without retirement contributions isn't as significant a deal as you might think. And if you have to use some of your future savings to get through this transitory time in life, no one (with a heart) will judge you for doing what's needed to make ends meet. Just be sure to understand what type of taxes you'll have to pay if you make an early withdrawal.

Typically, we don't withdraw from retirement funds until we're sixty to sixty-five years old. For that reason, if you withdraw money before that age, you may suffer up to a 10 percent tax. If possible, withdraw money from your non-qualified funds first, such as a Roth IRA in the US or a Tax-Free Savings Account (TFSA) in Canada.

WHAT IS THE RIGHT AMOUNT OF COVERAGE?

Once you're officially removed from your position, make sure that you protect yourself by exploring any health insurance (such as COBRA; see page 96) or other insurances you might be eligible for—even for the time being. This way, if something else happens to you, in addition to being out of work, you'll hopefully have enough of a security blanket to avoid further financial stress.

GETTING TO KNOW YOUR INSURANCE NEEDS

After a job loss, do your research to see if you can continue your benefits or coverage with the same plan out of pocket. If you can, double-check that the price fits within your budget, as employer benefits are typically costly outside of the group rate.

Don't be afraid to get multiple quotes and speak to numerous insurance professionals to ensure that you have the best possible price and coverage for your needs.

Insurance expert Kevin Bartel says the best way to know if you are speaking to a good agent is to ask: How do you get paid? If they answer the question directly and in one sentence or less, they're likely a good choice. But if they start giving you a long-winded explanation about the source of their compensation, it could be a red flag that the insurance agent is paid on commission.

Depending on the job loss you're facing, you may need a different approach to ensure that you are covered financially.

If you are laid off or furloughed from a full-time job and are single, it may be easier to adjust your expenses and lie low. However, if you are the breadwinner in your family, you may need to be more creative with your finances. Luckily, you should have access to some unemployment insurance in both of these situations to help cover some of your monthly expenses.

If you work part time and have your hours cut or are self-employed and live life on a roller-coaster income—meaning your income changes each month—an unemployment claim might not be as straightforward. Instead, consider looking for another job that can help you increase your earnings. It may not be your dream job—or even a great-paying job—but in worst-case scenarios, any income is better than nothing at all.

WHAT IF I DIDN'T LOSE MY JOB IN THE OBVIOUS SENSE?

Although most professional emergencies make us think of spending the unforeseen future browsing job postings, other experiences can force us to take a break from the workforce—such as injury (to both our body and our mind).

These days, hustle culture or a fast-paced work environment that encourages working long hours to achieve our goals can put a strain on our mental health. We're living through a time when we're expected to be accessible to our employers, and that we will respond to people more quickly than we can text. Professionally, it's exhausting to find the balance between working reasonable hours and still finding time to spend on our hobbies. Jefferson Bethke, author of *To Hell with the Hustle: Reclaiming Your Life in an Overworked, Overspent, and Overconnected World*, understands this reality all too well.

In his book, he says, "Our current hustle culture is no different; it's all about exceeding limits. It's about striving for that false freedom to do this. Eat that. Work this way. Just. Work. Harder. Network more. Just buy my masterclass and you, too, can be a millionaire by age nineteen."[11]

Recognizing these feelings of what most of us consider "burnout" is even more apparent for those who attempted to work through a global pandemic with little support and no childcare.

Amelia Vela was one of the many who felt the pressure to do it all, and from the outside, it looked as though she was doing well at managing life. But, in reality, she had no way to take care of herself between raising a toddler, managing the upkeep of her home, and working a full-time job. After being diagnosed with depression in November 2020, Amelia struggled to stay focused at work and began to fall behind. Finally, both her employer and her doctor concluded that the best option for her was to take a leave, using her short-term disability benefits.

This is a stark reality that many of us forget to consider. Approximately 25 percent of today's twenty-year-olds will become disabled.[12] Short-term disability can provide you with an income while you take a short leave of absence from work during an accident, illness, or hospitalization. However, it's always a good idea to check with your employer to see if this is an option for you before it becomes a necessity.

This type of leave wasn't Amelia's first choice, because the fear of leaving work for an extended period left her feeling more anxious than just working through it—but she had to put herself first.

I can relate to the fear of stepping back from something that our lives typically revolve around. It's a fear of feeling that you're not doing enough. A feeling of guilt or worry that nothing will change and taking time away is merely another setback that you can't afford to take.

But emergencies are just that—emergencies.

"Mental health issues are like carrying a bag of rocks on your back," says Amelia. "If your kid had to go through life with this huge, heavy bag of rocks and you could do something to lighten that load, you would do it, so why wouldn't you do it for yourself?"

But that doesn't mean the process of stepping back is easy, or possible, for everyone. Even as someone who has benefits and support from a medical professional, Amelia had to jump through hoops throughout the application process. If Amelia had to do this at her lowest point, she couldn't have possibly found the energy.

All of this is to say that even after filling out multiple forms, dealing with the back-and-forth between herself, her employer, and her bank, there is no guarantee that Amelia will receive approval. If she does, her benefits offer 67 percent coverage for the two to three months she'll be away from work.

From 2006 to 2015, only 34 percent of disability claims applications received approval. But 11 percent of those approvals still had to go through a reconsideration or appeals process.[13]

FAST FACTS
ABOUT SHORT-TERM DISABILITY:

▶ The most common coverage is 40 percent to 60 percent of your typical earnings.
▶ Your coverage will not kick in until two weeks after your leave begins.
▶ You may have to pay taxes on your short-term disability pay.

Is the process worth it? Amelia says that it absolutely is. If not for her recovery, for her daughter and partner.

If short-term disability isn't an option because you need more time away from your workplace, the second benefit to research is long-term disability. The most common long-term disability claims are for musculoskeletal disorders, such as carpal tunnel or tendonitis (29 percent); cancer (15 percent); and pregnancy (9.4 percent).[14]

IT'S OKAY TO ACCEPT THE LOSS
(AND IT'S OKAY TO WANT MORE)

Burnout happens—to all of us in one way or another. But sometimes we need to let ourselves rest and recover.

For most of us, job loss is an emotional experience. Not only does it impact our financial lives, but it takes us on a journey that often begins with self-reflection and asking ourselves if this is really the career for us. It's okay to use this time as a short period of growth and an opportunity to work on your financial and personal needs as a human being. We all need the space to accept this difficult transition in life—particularly when it wasn't something we ever thought would happen to us.

It's also okay to want to earn more money. Back in the 1980s, when neon was all the rage, Cabbage Patch dolls reigned supreme, and "E.T. phone home" was a popular catchphrase—life for twenty-somethings was pretty gnarly, dude. So let's try to paint a picture of life back in the eighties for those of us who have no idea where to start.

Imagine you're a super cute and bubbly twenty-five-year-old. You have been married for five years, live and love the dual-income-no-kids (DINK) life and spend a modest

7.5 percent of your income on your rent while living in the most popular area of the city that overlooks a beautiful river and a booming downtown.

Your outlook on life is carefree, you love to take road trips on the weekends, and you don't have a clue what you're doing with your money—but at twenty-five years old, you think, "What does it matter?" This was my mom's life just thirty-five short years ago.

Have you ever sat down with your parents and discussed money? Have you ever asked them for advice or wondered what they would do if they were in your financial situation? If not, you probably should.

Before having a lovely chat with my mom about her life around my age, my perspective about generational gaps was pretty misguided. Generally speaking, I knew that the cost of living was a lot lower and that the housing market was much easier to get into. However, I had no idea that we experienced the same confusion and lack of education regarding money. Only now, we can find that information within seconds, whereas our parents had to seek guidance from the people in their network.

When I asked my mom about her salary, wage, or working life during her twenties, she joked about how she was likely making more back then than she does now. However, within five minutes, we both felt sick to our stomachs upon realizing that stagnant wages are still the norm and that some people are still trying to get by, making what my twenty-five-year-old mom was making over thirty-five years ago.

At her first job, my mom made $15 an hour (more than the current minimum wage where I live) and at her first career, she was bringing in around $1,700 per month. My first job working in the food-service industry paid $9 an hour and in my first career, I was bringing in $2,900 per month.

Although it certainly looks like an increase, salary-wise, that $1,200 bump doesn't amount to much when you consider how much it cost to live in 1980, compared to how much it costs to live today. Any simple inflation calculator can tell you that $100 in 1980 would equal $329.73 in 2021.

Both of my parents are Baby Boomers—so, you can imagine the fun we have debating life now versus life then and also (of course) who did it better. However, conversations like the one my mom and I decided to tackle regarding finances are what helps us to understand each other on a different level. Without reflection on what our lives used to be and are now, we'd never really respect each other's challenges or successes as human beings.

So, for those of you who'd like to earn more—or feel that you should be earning more—you're likely not wrong.

When you accept your job, the last thing on your mind is whether or not someone else is getting paid more than you to do the same (or less) than what you will do. Most likely, you're more concerned with getting a consistent paycheck.

The annual income you take home varies based on a few factors, including your location, industry, and experience. Most often, though, salary ranges revolve around averages. So even as the hopeful employee going into a job negotiation, our value as an employee is typically based on those averages rather than our experience.

HOW CAN WE HELP EACH OTHER BECOME MORE THAN OUR AVERAGE SALARIES?

SAVE MORE MONEY, HOLD MORE POWER

The more money you have in your savings, the more power you hold. Imagine having an emergency fund so full you could start taking control of other areas in your life. For example, finally taking the leap into entrepreneurship. Or, better yet, leaving a toxic workplace and taking your time looking for a new position because you have a backup bank account that will help you accomplish all the things you've planned.

It's easier said than done when you live with averages, but even the smallest amount of security can create a security blanket that saves your financial future. When I first started saving, it was a weekly $20 transfer into a high-interest savings account that accumulated more quickly than I expected.

You're not in a race when it comes to money. There is always time to bounce back and better your financial life. Milestones are intimidating because we set deadlines for ourselves that no one else is facing. So, baby, let's walk. Not run. You have more time than you think.

INCREASE YOUR INCOME

Easier said than done, I know. Hearing this always makes my blood boil because if I could earn more money, I would—and so would you. Whether you can negotiate a raise, find a part-time job, or start your own income-producing business, increasing your pay will (obviously) make a drastic difference. As hard as it may be to spend your downtime working, it may also be well worth it in the long run.

But the natural way to increase your income is by advocating for yourself and others in the workplace. Look up average salaries online. Don't be afraid to share your income with fellow industry professionals (confidentially, because some companies frown upon this practice) to compare averages to determine if you're being paid fairly.

If you plan to ask for more money from your employer, there are a few ways to help prove your value. Research and track your progress over time at the company. Do your best to compile all positive feedback, ways you've helped the company earn revenue, and successful projects.

HOW CAN I NEGOTIATE FOR A HIGHER SALARY?

1. KNOW YOUR WORTH.

Build your confidence by researching your value based on experience, industry averages, and a solid understanding of your role. Knowing this makes it so much easier to ask for what you know you deserve.

2. GIVE A SPECIFIC NUMBER AT THE TOP OF YOUR RANGE.

This shows that you've done your research and increases your chances of getting a more significant raise.

3. SHARE YOUR ACCOMPLISHMENTS WITH YOUR BOSS AHEAD OF YOUR PERFORMANCE REVIEW.

Sharing your wins and growth as an employee a few weeks ahead of your performance review is key. This way, your boss has time to find out what, if anything, the company can offer you, leaving less need for negotiation.

4. ACT LIKE YOU'RE NEGOTIATING FOR SOMEONE ELSE.

Sometimes we get nervous advocating for ourselves, but if we imagine negotiating for a loved one, it can help us be more firm and less emotionally tied to the outcome.

COMMIT TO EDUCATING YOURSELF

You and I both know that, growing up, the amount of financial literacy offered in our educational system was minimal. If you want to become financially successful, one of the first steps is to understand the purpose of your money, how to best use it, and how to make your income work for you.

You are more than a number. Companies use salaries to reward our work ethic, intelligence, experience, and more. So let's be our own advocates for change. Prove why you deserve things, voice why you deserve a salary increase, and stay driven.

No matter how much you make, you decide how you use it. So whether you want to save half of your income, spend half of your income, or divide everything evenly among your budgeted categories, you will only be as financially successful as you choose to be.

Keep telling yourself that you deserve it, prove to others that you deserve it, and promise yourself that you will get there. Because you will—eventually.

The most important thing that you should gain from this section of the book is to remember how impactful a plan can be. The plan doesn't have to be perfect by any means. But it should provide you with some relief if and when you face an unexpected setback in your professional life.

TAKEAWAYS FROM THIS CHAPTER:

- ▶ Be aware of multiple income streams, and develop a bare-bones budget.
- ▶ Take advantage of the work compensation a company might offer—that is a part of your financial package! It is yours for the taking.
- ▶ If you cut back as much as you can and are still struggling financially, it's okay to do what you need to do to get by. For instance, don't worry about long-term savings when your goal is to put food on the table and keep a roof over your head.

5
HEALTH = WEALTH

LEARN TO NEGOTIATE BILLS
AND PROTECT YOUR WELL-BEING

SO FAR, MY MOST SIGNIFICANT MEDICAL EMERGENCY has involved my mental health. It's cost me the most money because it's not included in our publicly funded healthcare in Canada.

I have always had insurance through my full-time job. Still, even the coverage we receive through this option doesn't go very far in a year, especially if you need to regularly speak with a mental health professional. Often, I get uncomfortable writing about my journey with my struggles in places that I know are permanent—and it doesn't get more permanent than in a book. But, at the same time, it wouldn't be fair if I didn't acknowledge one of the most critical medical emergencies that exist today: our mental health.

I've touched on this topic a couple of times throughout the book, but I haven't told the whole story about my experience with depression, anxiety, and suicidal thoughts. All of which came crashing into my life in early 2017.

At the time, I was working at my full-time marketing job, doing all my typical daily activities, spending time with my now-husband, and finally feeling financially secure. And yet, I couldn't help but cry—daily. I struggled to find any bright spots in my days, which used to seem like such a simple concept. I hated commuting to a job that no longer inspired me, and I felt trapped in a cycle that no longer made me feel that life was worth living.

Each morning, I would get into my vehicle and drive the same route to work, in rush-hour traffic, over a bridge that spanned a river. At first, I would look at the water and think to myself, "I wonder what would happen if I drove my truck into the barrier?" Every week that passed, the story would get a little bit darker. "What if I drove off the edge of the road and injured myself just enough to get a break in the hospital? What if I went off the edge and didn't feel a thing? What if I wasn't here anymore? Would anyone miss me? What if I could just run away from everything happening in my life?"

Somehow, I had convinced myself that these thoughts were normal. I wondered, "Everyone considers suicide, right? Thinking about death is very common, isn't it?" And then one day, my friend Sarah called me and could sense that something was off. About fifteen minutes into our conversation, she asked me if I was thinking about suicide. The line went silent. We were both wondering what was going to come out of my mouth next. To no surprise, it wasn't words, just tears. "Oh my god," I thought to myself. "I have a severe problem."

Within seconds of getting off the phone, I booked myself an appointment with a therapist—and my journey to working on my mental health began. I've spent thousands of dollars meeting with therapists to work through my anxiety. Yet every dollar was worth it—because life is valuable.

You are important. And sometimes you need the time and the space to realize those things.

It can be helpful to think about the what-ifs without forcing yourself into an uncomfortable mindset. Everything we do to protect our body and mind is part of our lifelong financial decisions. And, no, I don't mean that eating a few too many ice cream sundaes was the wrong thing to do because I'd be *really* calling myself out here.

Instead, I mean that the longer you wait to start something or prepare for something that could somehow impact your earning potential or ability to provide for someone you love, the worse the problem is likely to get. And that decision will turn into a lesson.

The phrase "It will all work out okay" is never going to protect you from suddenly experiencing suicidal thoughts or a workplace incident. In fact, assuming you will never have to throw money at some sort of health issue is a bigger financial pipe dream than thinking you'll be able to support yourself in retirement by only investing in meme stocks.

But, as usual, being young can be enough to make anyone feel that they are invincible. For some people, not even serious injuries, hangovers, or a near-death experience can put them in the mindset that, in an instant, their lives could change forever.

Abigail Perry, founder of the personal finance blog *I Pick Up Pennies,* never got to experience feeling bulletproof. Instead, at just nineteen years old, she found out that she had a rare neurological disease called Guillain-Barré syndrome, otherwise known as an autoimmune disease that stops the brain from communicating with its nerves, paralyzing people to varying degrees.

What started with her toes going numb one morning ended with a three-month stay in the intensive care unit. Abigail had to completely step out of the American workforce only five years later to focus on her physical health.

She says she was one of the lucky ones to have her disability application approved. "For most people, the delay can take up to eighteen months." Instead, Abigail got her application approved in just a few months. But, of course, like most people who apply for disability insurance, it called for her to jump through quite a few hoops. She says that what she went through is fairly normal. After her initial application came a rejection, followed by an appeal, and, finally, a court hearing.

If you need disability insurance to cover your living expenses, Abigail encourages people to hire a lawyer right away. "They take 30 percent of your appeal, but it's worth it," she says, noting that they know exactly what to say to the courts to convince them that your need for insurance is legitimate. Because, yes, in most cases, they need convincing.

The healthcare system in the United States is complex, scary, and beyond expensive for anyone who isn't in picture-perfect shape. Even for those in great condition, an unexpected need for an ambulance can cost anywhere from $1,000 to $3,000 without insurance coverage. I mean, when you have a baby in a hospital, you come home with more than a crying newborn and a need for diapers. You'll also receive a $5,000 to $11,000 bill—if everything goes according to plan and you don't need any extra medical attention, that is.

In these situations, Abigail says it can almost be more difficult to repay your debt, since you can't guarantee a fixed income like disability insurance. Most people will have to continue to work a full-time job (or two) and slowly chip away at their medical debt. This is why, when people make comments about how irresponsible people are with their money, I like to remind them that it's not always a bad habit or a latte addiction. Instead, it's real-life emergencies that derail any financial progress we make. In fact, an investigation by the *Journal of the American Medical Association* proves this to be true, revealing that Americans are saddled with at least $140 billion in outstanding medical debt.[15]

CAN YOU NEGOTIATE YOUR MEDICAL DEBT?

When Abigail married her now-ex-husband, the two shared medical bills of around $12,000. But they had also been able to eliminate or reduce other medical bills through the hospital by doing a few different things. One option is applying for support through the financial aid department of the hospital. Depending on your income, the hospital will either reduce or eliminate the debt in its entirety. You can also do this for ambulance rides. Abigail says it's a simple process, including filling out a form and providing proof of income through a pay stub. Another option is to do what you can to negotiate with the hospital. "Most hospitals will work with you," says Abigail, encouraging others to realize that it's always worth the ask.

If you plan to negotiate your medical bill, the best route is to speak with a medical billing manager—and do so as soon as possible. The longer you wait, the more negatively impacted you will become financially. On the call, verify all of the details, including the cost, to ensure that you aren't overpaying. Just as we negotiate any bills, sometimes it can help do a bit of research to compare other prices. Although this might sound silly with healthcare, it's not a bad idea to confirm what other insurance providers are charging clients to see if you are getting a fair deal. Check online, call other insurance brokers to see what their rates are, or speak with friends and family who are insured elsewhere. Once you know, you can use these numbers as leverage.

Most medical debt, unfortunately, requires you to advocate for yourself or your loved one. Taking the time to call and negotiate different repayment options can make a huge difference in whether you pay the total amount or less than that. Ask if they have any repayment plans and whether they'd be willing to reduce the amount if you can pay a significant chunk up front. This is a great way to make use of an emergency fund. If they don't reduce the total, ask if they can at least remove the interest.

Negotiating isn't always easy, particularly if we're uncomfortable asking for help or speaking with someone we don't know. In these situations, don't be afraid to reach out to a non-profit consumer credit organization that might have debt negotiators to manage these calls on your behalf. You can also speak to someone who works in the medical industry, such as a nurse or administrator, who might be able to offer more insight into how you'd appeal or negotiate your debt load. Either way, if you are in a tough spot financially, asking for help is always an option—and you shouldn't feel ashamed that you need support for an essential bill.

THREE WAYS TO NEGOTIATE MEDICAL DEBT:

1. ASK FOR AN ESTIMATE BEFORE YOU RECEIVE MEDICAL CARE.

Although this isn't always an option, if you have a planned surgery, for instance, it's not a bad idea to get an estimate of what the procedure might cost. This way, you can also see if the bill matches (or comes close to) the estimate once you leave the hospital.

2. KEEP A LOG.

Either do it yourself or ask a loved one to keep track of everything during your stay at the hospital, from medications to the time you spend in each patient area. By doing this, you might be able to catch any errors, like duplicate charges or other inaccuracies on the bill for your stay. Sometimes these are honest mix-ups on the part of the hospital staff.

3. BRING YOUR OWN SUPPLIES.

If you are in need of something to make your stay more comfortable, rather than use the hospital supplies, don't be afraid to ask a friend or family member to pick up that item from the drugstore. It will likely cost half the price and still do the trick. Remember, you will be charged for everything the hospital provides to you.

Does it seem ridiculous to have to do all of this extra work during a medical emergency or hospital stay? Of course it does. But the reason we have to do this is because affordable healthcare isn't always as accessible as it should be. There is no shame in doing everything you can to reduce your medical debt. The type of help available may depend on your situation. For example, in the United States, if you are recently unemployed due to a reduction in hours, or due to a death or another serious life event, you might be able to use the Consolidated Omnibus Budget Reconciliation Act (COBRA). This federal law allows you to keep employee health insurance for eighteen or thirty-six months if you're willing and able to pay the premium yourself. COBRA covers spouses, ex-spouses, and dependent children, too, and some states offer mini-COBRA plans for companies not subject to the federal law. You may also be eligible for Medicaid, which is healthcare coverage for low-income Americans, pregnant women, seniors, and those with disabilities.

Of course, the best way to avoid having to negotiate medical costs is by having medical insurance to cover you in case of any healthcare emergency that may occur. According to the Centers for Disease Control and Prevention data, in 2019 there were 32.8 million Americans under age 65 without health insurance.[16] In addition, the Centers for Medicare and Medicaid Services data shows that in 2019, the average health spending for Americans was $11,582 per person.[17]

For a 40-year-old in 2021, the average health insurance premium cost $495 per month or $5,940 per year.[18] Insurance companies determine premiums based on the law, but can take into account your age, location, the number of people on your plan, and smoking or tobacco habits.

If you're one of the 32.8 million without coverage, having health insurance can be just as preventative as having an emergency fund—but having both is even better. This is because, even with health insurance, you will still need to cover your insurance deductibles, the same as you would for your home and auto insurance.

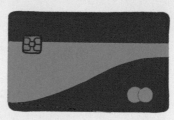

Typically, the lower your monthly insurance premium, the higher the deductible you'll have to pay out of pocket in any medical emergency. Deductibles exist to discourage people from using their insurance unless it's essential. Add up the deductibles for all your insurance policies to decide how much your emergency fund should hold.

Suppose you do have to use your health insurance. In that case, your insurance provider will likely cover your medical costs minus any co-payments or co-insurance. With co-payments, you pay a set dollar amount for general visits and prescriptions. With co-insurance, you cover a percentage of your medical costs alongside your provider.

Because most medical debt is unavoidable and not within our control, one of your only options may be to put the debt on a line of credit or credit card, and work to pay off your debt. You might also consider a personal loan. Before deciding, consider the interest you'll be paying, be confident that you can make at least the minimum monthly payment, and find out if your creditor or lender has anything to support medical debt repayment over typical consumer debt.

WHEN YOU CAN'T WORK
DUE TO A MEDICAL EMERGENCY

If you are in a situation where you cannot work due to a medical emergency, your options will vary depending on where you live. In Canada, for instance, you can apply for Employment Insurance sickness benefits for up to fifteen weeks. In the United States, things become a bit more complicated.

First off, the Family and Medical Leave Act (FMLA) will protect you if you need time off work to care for a sick family member or yourself. To qualify for FMLA, you need to have worked for your employer for at least a year, worked at least 1,250 hours or 24 hours per week, and your employer must have at least fifty employees within seventy-five miles of wherever you work.

If you qualify, you will receive up to twelve weeks of leave each year, and you can choose to take all twelve weeks off at one time or spread the time out throughout the year. But, keep in mind, this is unpaid leave. Your employer can choose to pay you (or not pay you) for this time off. This, again, makes the argument for an emergency fund and both short- and long-term disability insurance. FMLA leave is simply to protect you from losing your job or facing harassment.

WHAT IS CONSIDERED A MEDICAL LEAVE?

- ▶ A new child by birth, adoption, or fostering
- ▶ A serious health condition for yourself, a child, your partner, or a parent
- ▶ A chronic illness
- ▶ Pregnancy
- ▶ A drug or alcohol addiction

HOW CAN YOU TAKE THIS LEAVE AND NOTIFY YOUR EMPLOYER?

- ▶ Give your employer thirty days' notice or inform your supervisor as soon as possible
- ▶ Provide a doctor's note upon request by your employer.

Realistically, any time your health comes into play, the last thing you want to worry about is having to go to work. For that reason, financial independence and an emergency fund for *you* and *your needs* are the best forms of protection.

Many people wonder what they should do if the time away from work is unpaid, or if it's worth taking more than a few days off their job to see if that helps. In most situations, your best bet is to take the time to speak with a medical professional for guidance. Having an emergency fund to protect yourself exists for just these moments. You deserve to have the time away that you need to focus on your health and wellness.

It can feel like you're not doing enough or not working hard enough if a medical emergency forces you to sit on the sidelines after living a life that revolves around work—but the opposite is true. If you're resting, giving yourself time to heal, you're doing the only thing that actually matters.

WHAT ABOUT PET EMERGENCIES?

Of course, not all emergencies are the same, and sometimes we need to find ways to protect ourselves in other situations, such as when we incur costly medical bills for our furry friends, too.

Desirae Odjick, a financial writer, knows about this expense all too well. She had her dog, Jacob, for almost seven years when he was diagnosed with T-cell lymphoma, an aggressive cancer, at nine years old.

"The process of getting the diagnosis was one of the worst weeks of my life, and between the initial vet visit and a multiple-day stay at the emergency vet for diagnostic tests and treatments, just figuring out what was wrong cost us almost $4,000," says Desirae.

"When we got the final diagnosis, the vet walked us through what a chemo-based treatment plan could look like."

The vet shared that it would likely cost $12,000 to put Jacob through chemo for six months. Desirae and her partner felt it was a no-brainer to start treating a pet that was part of their family.

If you're thinking to yourself, "I could never afford a $12,000 emergency for myself, let alone that type of expense for a pet," you're not alone. But they could give such a committed yes because they had prepared—with pet insurance.

"Our emergency with Jacob showed me that when it comes to money, emotions matter just as much as the numbers," says Desirae. "You need to think about how you'll feel in an emergency and try to plan for how you're likely to react—not just how you'd like to react in an ideal world."

Desirae jokes that she wishes she was someone more rational—who could look at a $12,000 vet bill and say it was too much—but instead, she knows her emotional side will always take precedence.

HOW DO YOU MANAGE A PET EMERGENCY? HERE'S EXACTLY HOW, ACCORDING TO DESIRAE ODJICK, THE DOG LOVER:

GET A REALISTIC IDEA OF WHAT TYPE OF BILLS YOU'LL BE LOOKING AT.

Desirae says that cats, for instance, will have different common issues than guinea pigs. Shocking, I know! But seriously consider the fact that your specific breed of pet might also face common problems, like hip issues for German shepherds or increased cancer risk in golden retrievers. The best option is to ask friends and family who have owned similar pets and do a quick Google search to get a ballpark cost.

MAP OUT AN ANNUAL BUDGET FOR PET CARE, BASED ON YOUR RESEARCH.

Things like preventative medications, routine check-ups, and other recommended care are predictable. If you know the costs for the year, you can put an amount aside every month in preparation for your annual veterinary visits.

CHOOSE A PET EMERGENCY FUND, PET INSURANCE, OR BOTH.

An emergency fund for your pet is just as critical as one for a human. Even if you have insurance, you might need to pay up front for emergency care, and the provider might not cover your pet's condition. For example, a common exclusion is dental care for your pet. A tooth cleaning can run you hundreds of dollars or even more. Vet bills for more serious and worst-case conditions can run into five-figure amounts.

With any medical emergency, for humans or pets, insurance can be a product that not only provides a sense of financial security but also eases your mind. But, before purchasing any insurance, you must do your homework and research to determine that you have the best possible policy for you and your family. Health is a difficult emergency to prepare for, but if you have all of the right insurance and do the best you can to take care of yourself, mentally and physically, there is nothing more you can do to prepare and plan.

One of the biggest reasons it's important to advocate for yourself and your financial future is to have the freedom of choice and time. Having options when you don't feel your best, can't give your all, and need to rest is something that many people desire. When you have the financial means to protect your well-being, you are giving yourself so much more space to heal. Because having money doesn't just mean you have money. Having money means that you have security. It means that you have the freedom to make choices about how you spend your time. Having money is

an emotional security blanket that you cannot replicate—
and that is why saving and investing for your future self
is so powerful.

TAKEAWAYS FROM THIS CHAPTER:

▶ Mental health and physical health are both
medical emergencies that deserve time and
energy.

▶ Anytime you are faced with an unaffordable
medical emergency, remember to negotiate, no
matter what. Most hospitals and lenders are
willing to work with you, and, depending on
your income, you can receive an appropriate
discount.

▶ Whether the medical emergency is for you,
a family member, or a pet, you need an
emergency fund or insurance to cover these
surprise situations.

6

KEEP A ROOF OVER YOUR HEAD
HOW TO TAKE CARE OF YOUR MOST EXPENSIVE ASSET

SOMETIMES, IN LIFE, we have to accept that we can't always control how expensive things are. This is particularly true when it comes to keeping a roof over your head. In fact, possibly one of the most essential things in life *is* our ability to afford to put a roof over our heads.

We may not realize how amazing a feat that is, but it's something I'm constantly grateful for. These days, owning a home can feel like an unachievable milestone, given the current housing market. To pair that cost with an unstable economy can make it feel even more far off. Because, truthfully, whether you're a renter or an owner, the cost of living in a safe and comfortable space can be one of the most overwhelming aspects of our financial life.

But, and this needs to be said, whether you rent or own, a

home is still a home—and, for that reason, taking care of the place where you rest your head each night should always be a priority.

When we think of all the "financial emergencies" we face throughout our lifetime, most aren't true emergencies. Instead, they're inevitable expenses that we should be prepared to face. But, unfortunately, the only certainty in these unpredictable moments is that we can't be sure *when* they'll actually happen.

IS IT BETTER FOR YOUR FINANCIAL LIFE TO RENT OR TO OWN?

For me, renting was always the answer to how I would get ahead financially. Since I didn't start to invest until my mid-twenties, I figured that if I didn't have a mortgage, it would be easier to put cash away and focus on my retirement funds. Not to mention that I'd be avoiding the stress of the potential repairs, increase in mortgage rates, real estate crashes, and, well, the list goes on and on. "Sure, I face similar ups and downs with the stock market, but by the time I need that money, a rebound will hit," I thought. "Right?" Historically, yes.

Being a homeowner is a time-consuming job. There are always things to be updated, cleaned, and fixed. So why all of a sudden did I have a change of heart? Was it our leaky fridge, lack of office space, or the fact that our dinner table sits on a white carpet? I mean, who puts white carpet in a dining area? How can I trust myself with red wine? Answer: I can't.

The real reason is that, in some circumstances, home-ownership isn't always a better financial decision than renting. Shocking, I know!

At first, I questioned myself. Do I really want a home? Or was this just ingrained in my mind? Was I brainwashed as a young child to imagine this as the American Dream?

You see (and you know), growing up, I was told that owning a home one day would be inevitable. That owning a home was just another box I was supposed to check off in the game of life. "Can't I have all of these things renting, anyway?" I wondered. "Sure," was the answer. "I just might have to leave one day with not much notice and not many options."

The minute, literally, the minute I became a parent, renting no longer felt like the right choice for me. In my head, permanence and stability were floating around and fighting any brain cell thinking it would be funny to joke about a last-minute life change while soothing a crying newborn. Suddenly I became more grounded in where I am, who I'm with, and what I want: the three cornerstones of home-ownership. *Cornerstones coined by myself, that is.*

So, within eighteen months, we did everything in our power to save up a down payment and buy our forever home. We were in such a rush to find a place that we actually purchased our house without doing an in-person showing. We still felt it was the right choice, though I might not recommend it to everyone.

HOW DO YOU KNOW WHAT THE BEST CHOICE
IS FOR YOU?

Typically, there are three types of people when it comes to the rent-versus-own debate: (1) the people who live and die by homeownership, (2) the group of people who live and die by renting, and (3) the group of people who are like "Can't we all just do what's best for us and not argue because I'm tired and it's getting pretty repetitive?"

Then there are those who don't care that much but lean more toward owning and those who don't care that much but lean more toward renting. I'd say I'm on the "whatever is best for you" part of the spectrum, but I have my reasons for both renting and homeownership. After all, you are allowed to understand both perspectives.

One of the main things I like to tell people about renting and owning is that the final decision might be linked with your feelings about the future. What I mean by that is homeownership would probably work better for you if you know where you'd like to live for at least ten years and can envision settling down and living a much less "go with the flow" type of life. Why? Because I think we can all agree that homeownership is a lot less flexible than renting.

For example, as a renter, if the stove stops working or the drains are clogged, you can call your landlord and avoid the labor (and cost). But, as a homeowner, if your pipe bursts or the lawn needs mowing, those tasks are your responsibility and no one else's. This revelation brings me to my first point.

Homeownership in most major cities is much more expensive than renting. You can use your "I'd rather pay my mortgage than someone else's mortgage" reasoning all you want, but in many cases, unless you're rich or have a two-income household, homeownership is simply unaffordable. However, that doesn't prove much other than the fact that you really are more like your parents than you thought. Renting isn't throwing money away—especially if you're investing money in other ways for your future.

In fact, a large part of the reason that the wealth gap between generations is so vast is because of the unaffordability of housing. In 2019, Generation X held less than half as much wealth as Baby Boomers of the same age two decades earlier, and Millennials are on track to have even less.[19]

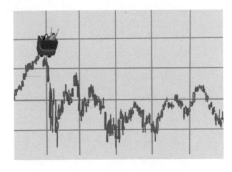

For that reason, thinking about the emotional side of owning is almost equally as important as the cost breakdown. Many financial experts will tell you that money management is 80 percent based on behavior and only 20 percent on knowledge. This sentiment is even more realistic when it comes to the rent versus own debate.

On that note, it's always good to remind people that you are allowed to move along the rent-versus-own spectrum, just as you are allowed to change your political views throughout your life. No one gets to tell you that you're a hypocrite for changing your mind—particularly when it doesn't directly affect them.

Before buying, we would regularly watch the market, discuss our wants, and put away large chunks of our paychecks to reach our goal. Talking about buying a home was a four-year conversation. If you plan to make a major purchase, like a home, with another person, you have to have tough conversations: in-depth discussions about the down payment, emergency funds, your maximum budget, and then, of course, lifestyle expectations.

Possession day came and went, and in an instant, our cost of living went up by nearly 80 percent—and that's not even a joke. Not everyone can relate to a rise in monthly costs when they take on homeownership, and I wish I could say the same, but it just wasn't possible to keep our expenses as low as they were when we were renters. We fully anticipated the increase in monthly expenses, but that doesn't mean it didn't take some adjusting and some readjusting before we had all of our bills taken care of.

Less than one year later, we managed our budget as homeowners with no problems, yet not without a few hiccups. Household emergencies are a perfect example of anticipated emergency expenses. We invest in an asset that requires annual maintenance. Every appliance in our home has a shelf life. Our roof will certainly need replacing every ten to fifteen years.

For those who did face a financial emergency in 2019, the cost wasn't exactly a quick fix. Three out of ten adult

Americans surveyed said that their largest unexpected expense cost $5,000 or more.[20]

So, in these situations, it's important to think of household emergencies as planned expenses instead. What many of us fail to recognize is that the cost of homeownership doesn't stop as soon as you cough up a down payment and secure a mortgage. Instead, the expenses of owning property are ongoing as we live in the homes we love.

If you're here in the midst of one of those expenses, don't panic. Now is the perfect time to start to set yourself up to afford those costs in the future—whether in six months or six years from now. The question everyone always wants to know when I explain to them the importance of saving for a household emergency fund is: How much? It's a valid question, and I admire your curiosity.

Just two weeks to the day after taking possession of my first home, my high-end stove stopped working. It was an unexpected expense that no one wants to deal with, particularly after dumping all of their savings into a down payment and closing costs just to get the keys to their new home. Luckily, it was "just" a $500 repair. But the even luckier part of this story was that we had enough of a buffer in our savings to cover that cost instead of putting it on our credit card and starting our first month as homeowners in the red.

Something I've always done is save enough money to cover the cost of replacing our most expensive appliance, and I add a sort of contingency fund—or buffer. We made the choice to save $10,000 in a household emergency fund,

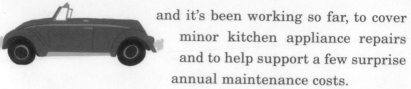

and it's been working so far, to cover minor kitchen appliance repairs and to help support a few surprise annual maintenance costs.

Another option when it comes to determining how much you should save for a household emergency fund is what the "experts" will tell you—and that is to save 1 percent to 5 percent of the purchase price of your home to cover these surprise expenses.

But when I asked Romana King, real estate expert and author of *House Poor No More*, if this was a realistic number, she immediately debunked the idea.

"We give this advice because we have no other answer," says Romana. "In this situation, people who purchased thirty years ago are not saving enough, and people who purchased now are saving too much." She says that if you are following this rule, you are leaving way too much money on the sidelines doing nothing for you.

Instead, Romana says that what we spend on maintenance each year, which is in the ballpark of $3,000 to $5,000, should be what we save to account for our planned household expenses, such as repairs and appliance replacements. You'll spend a portion of this money each year, but you'll accrue some money from simply saving up for these planned expenses.

Romana says, "People love rules, but I think the rule in this situation is just to have a goal." Instead of worrying about how much of a cushion you have, the focus should be on the habits that help you save for that cushion.

WHAT IF A HOUSEHOLD EMERGENCY HAPPENS
AND I DON'T HAVE ANY SAVINGS?

If putting money into yet another emergency fund doesn't sound like your style, and your risk tolerance is high, there are other options. One of those options is a Home Equity Line of Credit (HELOC). As a homeowner, you have access to additional leverage that renters don't have. HELOCs can be a great stopgap emergency fund for homeowners. You can use this type of credit to borrow against your home. It's a straightforward way to access credit that you can repay over time, with low interest and at a later date.

But, keep in mind, using a line of credit to cover emergencies can be a risky move if you're not in a good financial position—you could lose your home if you can't pay back the debt—or if you don't like to leap before looking. This leap comes because we can't predict the future. So, before you decide to skip saving for household emergencies, ask yourself if you can handle another monthly payment on top of your current bills, particularly if you lost your job tomorrow.

Although we don't always like to admit it, many homeowners tend to live beyond their means without realizing it. So do your part to take inventory and get to know whether this is a feasible plan for you before crossing your fingers and jumping in with a blindfold on.

Romana and her husband are big believers in property ownership, not just as an asset to own, live in, and passively build net worth, but as a way to actively grow the asset side of their ledger. A HELOC allows them to invest their money in other ways, and use their line of credit to cover larger household expenses, like a roof replacement.

HOW DO YOU KNOW IF A HELOC IS A GOOD OPTION FOR YOU?

▶ You can adjust your spending habits and budget to repay the debt on a dime.

▶ You are confident in your ability to earn a livable income.

▶ You are highly motivated to repay debts as quickly as possible. If you suddenly face a significant household expense, like a major toilet clog (I won't ask) that requires a professional plumber, but you don't yet have an emergency fund, there are still other ways to avoid complete financial disaster.

Financing certain debts using a personal loan or line of credit can be a great way to create a more manageable payment plan, rather than putting the entire cost of the fix or appliance on your credit card. Some of the benefits include low interest rates for repayment, accessibility, and they enable you to get the repair done without having to wait—which sometimes makes life a lot easier.

But there are some considerations and need-to-knows before you sign on the dotted line. For starters, many of these loan applications require a hard inquiry on your credit, which can cause a slight reduction in your credit score. Although that may not be a big deal to some, it could make the difference between landing a place to live or financing another (more pressing) need.

Second, it's essential to read the fine print any time you take on more debt. Although the purchase may come with zero interest for twenty-four months, it could come with fees on the side that you may not have anticipated.

If you find that the contract doesn't sound like a good fit, ask yourself about the urgency in fixing the "emergency" today. If your dishwasher stops working, would it be better to self-finance and save for the item over the next few months? Or are you in dire need of a way to keep your dishes clean immediately?

A significant part of the reason we spend money is that we can feel shame if we don't have the same lifestyle as our family or friends. Therefore, the lines between an essential purchase and a non-essential purchase can blur together, making us forget our priorities. Don't feel obligated to make a purchase if it's not life or death.

WHAT ABOUT REAL UNEXPECTED HOUSEHOLD EMERGENCIES?
THE ONES THAT NONE OF US CAN PREDICT . . .

This is an equally important question. How do you guard against the unplanned, like a house fire or a hailstorm? The answer here is simple: You need insurance. An insurance policy is an interesting part of our financial life because, for many, it's not a choice. If you are going to make a six-figure purchase, like, say, on your dream home, your lender will require you to cover that expense with insurance. Not to mention, it's there to protect you when something comes completely out of nowhere to throw off any progress you may have made with your money.

Imagine driving home from work and suddenly experiencing a massive hailstorm. Cars begin to pull under bridges in hopes of avoiding getting hit. By the time you arrive at home, you realize that your roof has sustained significant damage, and your attic is flooded. Rather than panic (more than you already are), you know that you have the right coverage to make you feel as though the hail damage never happened just one or two weeks later. Your insurance policy is a security blanket that we all need in moments of high-stress and high-anxiety situations.

Even renters can face these expenses, although they may not be as significant in number. Romana says that most of us undervalue what we cannot see. For renters, the idea that because the property is not theirs can lead to a false assumption that their personal belongings are easy and affordable to replace. In reality, that's not the case. She says one of the best ways both owners and renters can protect themselves is through homeowner's or tenant's insurance.

> **SPOILER ALERT**
> A HOME COSTS MORE THAN THE MORTGAGE

HOW DO YOU TAKE INVENTORY OF WHAT YOU OWN?

Walk around your apartment and start to add up the cost of replacing all your belongings—the big stuff like your brand-new washing machine and fifty-inch TV, and the little stuff like socks and underwear. In as few as fifteen minutes, the tabulation should leave you shocked—it would cost a lot of money to replace your stuff. Probably a lot more money than you have in the bank right now. That sort of loss is what tenant's or homeowner's insurance covers: sudden, unexpected, large losses that would cripple you financially if you had to pay for them out of pocket.

Getting tenant's insurance is a win-win-win. It's a small and manageable monthly payment that can protect you from statistically improbable events, but financially disastrous debts.

Dealing with one of these disasters in your home can be overwhelming, but there are only a few steps you need to remember during a crisis situation. First, make sure that you have access to a digital copy of your insurance policy. This way, you'll always be able to access that document to refer back to if necessary.

FOUR KEY STEPS TO FILING A HOMEOWNER'S INSURANCE CLAIM:

1. Get evidence of all the damage digitally, using photos and videos to submit to your insurance company.

2. Once you know the cost of the damage by speaking with contractors or industry professionals, call your insurance provider to open a claim. If you can confidently say that the damage is more than you'd have to pay for your deductible, call the insurance company first.

3. Keep track of the details, as you will need to know where and what happened, as well as the approximate dates and times that the damage took place.

4. Wait to hear from an insurance claims adjuster to oversee your file or assign a contractor to begin repairs.

HOMEOWNERSHIP IS EXPENSIVE IN MORE WAYS THAN YOU MIGHT EXPECT

Aside from insurance, another real unexpected household emergency that so many people deal with is lifestyle inflation—or another famous idiom, Keeping Up with the Joneses. So many times, when we move into a new place or home, or, hell, even when we get a promotion at work and keep everything else in our life the same, we feel a weird sense of obligation to match the way we live to that financial change.

When you buy a new home, you need new furniture, cute home decor, and a fresh coat of paint. In addition, you need to match your neighbor's perfect front garden and maybe even their luxury vehicle that's always sitting in the driveway. At least, that's how we feel and how we're programmed as consumers. It can also be real pressure, with some neighbors applying pressure to conform to ensure the value of the homes in their community aren't impacted.

Turns out, I could relate. It's tough to control the urge to raid every home decor store within a ten-mile radius. Never had I ever looked at a table runner and thought to myself, "This will be perfect for the first time I host Thanksgiving"— until I had my own space.

Homeownership turns you into a shopaholic. No, seriously. You want every little corner of your home to be perfect. Every wall needs to be decked out with an art piece. Every kitchen appliance needs to be top of the line. I've had to retrain myself to resist the urge to spend.

After all, I think spending five figures on a down payment is probably enough for a while. You don't want to let lifestyle inflation creep in just because you finally allowed yourself to spend some of your savings.

The best way to control this financial emergency is to stop buying for the Joneses and start buying for yourself. In her book *Untamed*, Glennon Doyle says it best:

"Every time you're given a choice between disappointing someone else and disappointing yourself, your duty is to disappoint that someone else. Your job throughout your entire life is to disappoint as many people as it takes to avoid disappointing yourself."[21]

That is the one piece of advice I wish I'd had when I moved into my first rental, and definitely when I bought my first home.

Sometimes, though, it's too late, and we're already living beyond our means in a home or rental we can't afford. Instead of panicking, there are a few things to try before you sell or break your lease.

Step one is to take a serious look at your expenses. Although annoying to review constantly, the cost of living is always the first place to go anytime you're struggling financially. For example, it's best to itemize and review your spending over the last six months to a year when it comes to a steep mortgage or rent. Then, you can find out your actual expenses and reduce your discretionary spending as much as possible.

If that doesn't do the trick, because it's not always easy to spend less when we're already spending as little as we can, it might be time to find another roommate to generate more income as a homeowner or reduce your monthly rent as a tenant. Keep in mind that, as a renter, your lease will stipulate who the tenants are. So, it's best to get the landlord's approval to add a new roommate. Otherwise, you may breach your contract.

The last option for homeowners is to restructure their mortgage with a lower interest rate or extend their amortization period. For a quick example, shifting a $500,000 mortgage amortized over twenty-five years, rather than twenty years, can significantly reduce your monthly payment. Keep in mind, though, the apparent downside in this scenario is extending your mortgage repayment by five years, causing you to pay more interest over your mortgage term.

If you've exhausted all your options, it's okay to sell or move out. Sometimes we over-commit and overextend ourselves to live in a space we fell head over heels in love with. Protecting your home and the belongings within it doesn't have to be as stagnant or unambiguous as saving for job loss. Instead, you have a variety of options to control these costs without letting them take your financial progress and turn it into a struggle.

TAKEAWAYS FROM THIS CHAPTER:

▶ Whether you rent or own, you need to have the proper insurance to protect your belongings.

▶ A good benchmark for savings can be your most costly appliance or to save the current average maintenance cost on a home, which hovers around $3,000 to $5,000 per year.

▶ There are many options to leverage debt as a homeowner, which can sometimes be the best way to maintain and protect your property.

7
WHEN A TORNADO STRIKES
DEALING WITH THE FINANCIAL
SIDE OF EMERGENCY PREPAREDNESS

SUPPOSE YOU'RE HALFWAY THROUGH this book and starting to think to yourself, "Wow! How many more things do I need to prepare for, and is money really *this* terrifying?" First, I want to remind you of who you're dealing with.

Hi. It's me! The woman who says you need three emergency funds.

(But seriously. You should have three emergency funds.)

One day, while finishing a podcast interview and joking with a friend about how anxious I am about all the things that can go wrong in life—and with our money—she told me that instead of telling people I was paranoid, it would be better to say to people that I was risk averse. "It sounds more appealing," she laughed. To which I agreed.

And so, in this chapter, when I start blabbing on about all the natural disasters and potential emergencies we can face in our society, I'm going to lean into being that risk-averse professional. Who instead uses being conservative with money as a strength rather than a weakness. Because, honestly, emergency preparedness matters. A lot.

In 2021, a house fire a few streets over from ours sent shock waves through the community. Two families were inside when it happened, and seven people died. While the cause was never released, I wasn't surprised. I knew after doing my research that there are more than 350,000 home fires each year and that within two minutes, a fire can be life-threatening. Within five minutes, an entire home can become engulfed in flames.[22]

After having a kid and buying a home, I always wanted to ensure that all of my bases were covered. So we immediately bought a fire extinguisher, fire ladder, and fire blanket for the upstairs in our home. We sat down, mapped out a plan, and put together an emergency kit for unexpected and quick-exit situations. Then we purchased a fire-safe box for all of our essential documents, such as estate plans and homeownership papers.

And to answer your question, because, yes, I know what you're thinking: I am an absolute blast at parties.

Having an emergency kit and an emergency preparedness plan is essential for your health and safety and your financial security. Going over these types of backup plans can help you manage your cash on hand and your food supply without going over the top or overspending.

Although it's not any fun to consider these types of disasters, the reality is that they are more common than we realize. Not only do they require emergency preparedness but they also have significant financial implications. For that reason, it's critical to know how to manage the money side of a natural disaster.

During 2020, a time when a global pandemic made us repeatedly ask ourselves whether life could get any worse, multiple natural disasters hit communities. They pushed people into an even more uncomfortable and difficult place in life.

Less than a year earlier, we had moved to Calgary from Fort McMurray, and thankfully so. Unfortunately, in June 2020, a devastating flood left our previous rental unit under water, along with hundreds of other properties. In addition, our friends from the community were left without a home for nearly two months due to hazardous materials that can inundate a property during a flood. Not to mention, the city had been decimated by a forest fire in May 2016. Tina Kuhr was one of the displaced residents in Fort McMurray for both the fire and the flood.

The fire was her first experience with emergency preparedness for a natural disaster. She and her partner had just gotten the keys to their first home three weeks before the mandatory evacuation and were lucky it wasn't touched by the fire. Despite having to evacuate for nearly six weeks, she and her partner were extremely fortunate to continue to receive financial support from their employers. But Tina knew that this was not the case for all evacuees. The fire made her rethink her emergency fund if a natural disaster were to ever happen again—and then it did. This time, they weren't as lucky.

The flood hit them financially in a major way. Not only were they displaced from their home for another six weeks, but this time, their home didn't survive unscathed. Water filled their basement and damaged parts of their main floor. For Tina, the most significant financial impact from both natural disasters was the resale value of their home.

"Many of our neighbors gave their keys to the bank because the value of our homes has declined nearly 40 percent over five years," Tina said. This decline comes with a rapid economic downturn and multiple natural disasters. At the time, Tina had flood insurance, but since the recent damage, every single insurance company has refused to provide coverage for her home—making it even harder to sell.

THREE WAYS TO PREPARE FOR DISASTER

1. EXPECT THE UNEXPECTED

You can never save too much in your emergency fund. So even though you think it may never happen to you, Tina says it's better to prepare. During the flood evacuation, she was thirty-eight weeks pregnant, and fortunately, she was ready.

2. PACK AN EMERGENCY KIT

The forest fires were Tina's first experience with a disaster, and she says she was brutally unprepared to evacuate for six weeks. All they had time to grab was a couple of water bottles. She encourages others to keep their emergency documents together, pack an emergency kit, and save up for emergency expenses, especially if you live near a flood zone

WHAT TO PACK IN YOUR EMERGENCY KIT:

- ▶ Your emergency plan
- ▶ Enough water for seventy-two hours
- ▶ Non-perishable food
- ▶ A first aid kit
- ▶ A rechargeable flashlight or matches and a candle
- ▶ Small bills and change
- ▶ A change of clothes and a warm blanket
- ▶ A whistle or noisemaker
- ▶ A small tool kit
- ▶ Personal protective equipment

Keep in mind, you should keep important documents, such as an estate plan or the deed to your home, in either a flood or fireproof box, a safe deposit box at the bank, or in a secure cloud storage account online.

3. STAY CALM AND ACCEPT HELP

When friends and family offer to help you, always accept the help. Tina and her partner were fortunate to stay at friends' and families' homes during their evacuation and had enough insurance coverage to stay in hotels if needed. Either way, options are essential in an emergency, and you don't need to feel guilty for taking advantage of a free bed or couch.

Tina also recommends keeping a full tank of gas or keeping a full gas can in a shed on your property. If your vehicle's tank isn't full, a few gallons in a can will help. You never know when you'll need to go in a hurry.

Aside from Tina's list, four essential tips to help you assemble the best possible emergency plan include prevention, preparation, response, and recovery.

To help prevent an emergency, get to know what potential risks exist in your city or neighborhood. From there, you'll have a better idea of the ways you can protect yourself and your home.

To prepare for unexpected disasters, consider printing an evacuation checklist, depending on what potential emergencies you might face. Then put together an emergency kit and an evacuation plan, advising your family members of the best possible escape route should there be any rush, and include tips on what to do in each of these situations. Practice the escape plan to make sure it works.

When we're in a real emergency, it's hard to focus on anything other than getting to safety. But, because you already took preventative measures and made a plan, it should be a bit less overwhelming to respond appropriately. Listen to trusted authorities and follow all evacuation requirements.

Lastly, once you finally have time to recover from an emergency, the most important thing is to focus on your physical and mental health. Sometimes, even though we do everything we can to prevent disaster, we still have to rebuild.

In Austin, Texas, my friend and fellow financial expert

Kara Pérez saw many of her loved ones displaced due to the extreme cold they were experiencing in a city that wasn't built for any temperature below zero.

The disaster left people without electricity, water, internet, or heat for two weeks. In total, 111 people lost their lives, and, unfortunately, most of those deaths were preventable.

In a genuine emergency, rarely are we thinking about money. If we walk through a forest and come across a bear, we know that our ridiculously perfect budget and fully funded emergency savings will not be enough to get us out of this situation. In moments like these, Kara says the immediate reality of facing our humanity—and realizing that we aren't invulnerable—comes to the fore.

"The more money you have, the more immune you are to social problems," says Kara. "You can pay for a parking ticket, you can buy your way out of whatever—but you cannot buy your way out of negative temperatures."

One thing that this disaster taught her is that cash is still essential. "It's understandable to think you don't need it because a lot of the world is digital," says Kara. "But if the power goes out, you can't swipe your credit card."

Kara thinks that for most upper-middle-class people, it's easy to become removed from your own money. "You need to get close and personal with your money and make sure that you have everything you need." These disasters complicate our lives like nothing else we face because we can't predict the outcome and can control only so much. It is easier to forget and move on than to anticipate the same disaster happening twice or another major catastrophe.

IS THIS GOING TO KEEP HAPPENING?

It's hard to imagine that this isn't our new reality. Especially since the 2021 United Nations Intergovernmental Panel on Climate Change report was over 4,000 pages long. One line read: "Human-induced climate change is already affecting many weather and climate extremes in every region across the globe."[23] That statement alone can make us all feel like we should be doing more to prevent, prepare, and plan for our new reality. But can the average person even do that? Tanja Hester, the author of *Wallet Activism*, thinks so.

She says the best thing we can do to make a difference and prepare for the climate crisis is to follow the money. "Most people talk about responsible investing, but they forget to mention responsible banking," says Tanja. "I think responsible banking is almost more important."

The Rainforest Action Network found that since 2015, the world's sixty biggest banks have financed fossil fuels by nearly $3.8 trillion.[24] By using financial institutions that invest their money in industries that damage our environment, we are giving them the funding they need to continue contributing to our issues. Instead, Tanja says to look for credit unions or socially responsible banks that continue to become more common. Although it might seem like a pain to transfer or switch banks, it's worth it. Tanja says that even if just 10 percent of a big bank's customer base withdrew their money in favor of a bank that is more environmentally conscious, they'd consider making the necessary changes to do better for our world.

The second thing we average people can do is to hold onto what we already have. When Tanja suggested this idea, I immediately thought about minor things, like jars or clothing, but she says the more important things matter, too. Things like keeping a car longer or staying in the same house longer are beneficial. All of these significant assets cost a lot of money to reproduce new, and if they're still working—even if they burn fossil fuel—it's a lot better to avoid the impact of producing something else entirely.

Lastly, advocating for policy action and voting for leaders who acknowledge the importance of change can be the most impactful way to alleviate the climate crisis. "Go to meetings, elect the right officials," says Tanja. "A little bit of consumer action can make a big difference."

When I asked her if the climate crisis should be considered a financial emergency, she didn't hesitate to agree. Tanja says severe weather events can cause worldwide disruption—which we saw when COVID-19 and several natural disasters struck simultaneously, causing food and supply shortages. These types of disturbances make everything more expensive, and it's likely those types of events will become more common.

ProPublica and the *New York Times* put together an analysis of how climate change may impact much of the world over time. They found that by 2050, "parts of the Midwest and Louisiana could see conditions that make it difficult for the human body to cool itself for nearly one out of every 20 days in the year."[25]

The weather changes will also make it challenging to grow food, and we will also see rising sea levels. The analysis states that "these factors will lead to profound economic losses—and possibly mass migration of Americans away from distress in much of the southern and coastal regions of the country."[26] Tanja says the more that we can expect and prepare for these changes, the better. "I know it's tough advice to give to someone who doesn't have a lot saved or is just starting, but I don't think pretending that it's not true helps anybody, either."

HOW DO I AVOID BECOMING A DOOMSDAY PREPPER?

So, preparing is vital. But the problem with this is how do we find the line and know where to stop? Bridget Casey, founder of Money After Graduation and a financial expert, grew up only knowing a life of overpreparation.

When her dad remarried a devout Mormon, the church was very adamant that each household keep a year's worth of food in storage. In Utah, where she grew up, she says that they build houses with this type of storage in mind.

"The teachings of the church are that you should always be prepared because you're actually preparing for the apocalypse," says Bridget. "It sounds silly, but they also teach that this practice can help your family in the case of job loss or an illness."

Since learning that her upbringing isn't typical, she now does her best to find balance in preparing just enough for her food supply, toiletries, and cash on hand without

going overboard. "I don't keep a year's worth of food on hand, but I do keep enough food for three months and toiletries for six months."

For her, it's a habit, and, in part, she thinks, because she grew up in poverty. Now, as an entrepreneur, she also knows what it's like to have an inconsistent income. So it makes sense to stock up to avoid the stress and worry should something happen.

During the start of the pandemic, when most people were rushing to the grocery store to stock up on water and food or spoke about increasing or bulking up their emergency funds, she says it felt good that she was already prepared.

Knowing that this might not be the last pandemic, economic downturn, or emergency that we experience, Bridget says the best thing anyone can do to prepare for these situations is to find some comfort in flexibility. Because that will be way more valuable than trying to ensure that your life always stays the same.

"I think that is often the context behind preparedness," says Bridget. "We think, 'How can I make sure my life always stays the same even though everything changes around me,' and I don't think that's good." But, of course, she's not wrong—and honestly, she rarely is—that's why she's one of my best friends in the personal finance world.

Most of us expect that things will return to the way they always were after any type of emergency. We think carrying hand sanitizer and staying home when we have a runny nose is only a temporary part of life, rather than permanent. We're unwilling to accept that events and a quick outing to the grocery store may never feel the same as it did before COVID-19.

We joke that there will be a "new normal," but none of us really believe things will stick. We're too caught up in living life the way we're used to and being comfortable in our routines.

But the thing is that when an emergency strikes or our town is hit with a tornado, it doesn't go back to the way it was. Instead, we make improvements or change completely—and most of us are never the same again. We lived through something we didn't plan for, which can make us more anxious and more fearful of what else can happen in our lifetime.

The good news is that we can do a few things to protect ourselves aside from building an emergency fund and packing an emergency backpack. We can insure, insure, insure!

For one thing, having homeowner's insurance can cover a wide variety of damage. The coverage can vary from interior damage, like flooding in a basement due to a burst pipe, to exterior damage, like roof or siding damage after a hailstorm.

But if insurance no longer becomes an option, as Tina experienced in Fort McMurray, the better thing to do is avoid buying in areas that are considered flood zones, fire risks, or where the climate crisis might come knocking first.

You can get insurance to protect more than your four walls. For example, there is life insurance, disability insurance, renter's insurance, and car insurance. All of these measures are important, depending on your situation, and it's never a bad idea to look into each of them if you feel you could have more (or better) coverage. And, depending on where you live, some insurance might be required by law.

If you are put in a situation where you can't return to your home for a few weeks or even months because of damage, or you have to replace nearly all of your possessions, there are a few key things to remember.

During evacuations, if you are in the United States, FEMA's website at www. ready.gov provides emergency preparedness tips and the FEMA smartphone app lists open shelters during an active disaster. Text SHELTER and your zip code to 43362 to sign up for emergency alerts, and by texting PREPARE to 43362, you can get monthly preparedness tips. For non-governmental help, visit the American Red Cross at www.redcross.org. If possible, look to family or friends who are in a safe zone and can provide shelter.

If you are in Canada, you can contact the Canadian Red Cross at www.redcross.ca/prepare, the St. John Ambulance at www.sja.ca, or the Salvation Army www.SalvationArmy.ca.

If you are driving to an evacuation shelter or hotel, be sure to look at reports for road closures and ensure that the hotels have vacancies or the ability to take in new guests.

Out of all the potential financial emergencies we face, the ones that happen the least often are the ones we feel we don't need to prepare for—or that we can't prepare for. But, in reality, it's the opposite. There are always ways to help prevent disaster and protect yourself, which I try to remind myself and others of regularly.

You don't need to walk through your day consumed by thoughts about the sky falling. But you do need to understand that most of these natural disasters you see on television and social media, that we're mostly desensitized to, are not impossible scenarios.

▶ Preparing for natural disasters should be front of mind because, unfortunately, climate change isn't going anywhere.

▶ You need to have insurance for your home, an emergency kit for surprise evacuations, and cash on hand for power outages and quick exits.

▶ You can prepare without overpreparing or becoming a doomsday prepper. Get to know what disasters are likely in your area and map out a plan from there. Preparation is your best weapon.

8

EXPECT THE UNEXPECTED

HOW TO TAKE CARE OF FAMILY AND DEAL WITH DEATH

SOMETIMES, WE CAN DO EVERYTHING to prepare for life's ups and downs, and, still, we'll manage to be caught off guard when we least expect it. It's happened to me a few times, and I'm sure it's happened to you, too. The most memorable financial challenge I dealt with happened *before* I knew that planning ahead was essential.

It was the tail end of 2017, and I was just starting to feel like I had a handle on my financial life. I had paid off my debt and was regularly investing for my future. My husband and I had been married for one year, and he had just accepted a new job in a city seven hours away from where we grew up. So a lot was changing, but we felt like we were ready for the growth.

The next thing on my list of financial goals was to increase my income, and it just so happened that I got my dream job offer with a slight raise and the ability to work remotely. It was an easy decision to say yes. But just two weeks after accepting a new job offer, something felt off. It wasn't the work, though.

Instead, I realized I hadn't had my period in two months. How could I have not noticed this? Of course, that is exactly what you're thinking right now, and what I was whispering to myself in the bathroom mirror. Between the move, the back-and-forth visiting friends and family, and the difficulty of trying to acclimate to a new community, it didn't even cross my mind. It wasn't like me to be late, but at the same time, I figured it could be from the mass amounts of stress I was facing.

Just in case, I thought it would be safe to take a pregnancy test. I was so sure that it wouldn't be positive, I didn't tell anyone—not even my husband. I whipped over to the local drugstore, grabbed the first test I could find, embarrassed for no reason, and paid for the pee stick.

I took the test immediately upon getting home and wasn't even anxious as I waited the three minutes for the result to appear. But when I flipped over the pregnancy test, there it was, glaring at me. Two bold pink lines. Pregnant. Me. Pregnant. At twenty-seven. Pregnant. With a new job. In a new city. With no plan. Pregnant.

Usually, when women find out this news, they're either jumping for joy or terrified. I was the latter. We hadn't planned for this, talked about this, or even considered this might happen—especially now, when everything in life finally felt like it was falling into place.

But isn't that what an emergency is? Something you least expect, and at the most inconvenient of times? That's what this felt like, anyway. It was my first financial lesson in how to anticipate the things you don't see coming. Instead of buying the famous book *What to Expect When You're Expecting*, someone really needs to give new parents a guide that goes over what to expect when you're unexpecting.

> *Having a family is hard, and it's expensive*
> *in more than one way. It's not just diapers*
> *and college funds. It's also emotionally taxing*
> *and can make your professional life more difficult.*

For women, having a baby can be a financial emergency because we have to choose whether we can balance work and life if we don't have all of the privileges a mother needs to be successful. Women need time off to recuperate and to be there for their child when they're sick, have an appointment, or, say, a global pandemic shuts down their daycare or classroom.

Statistically, mothers suffer what some call the "motherhood penalty." We are perceived to be less competent and less committed to our careers. Yet, employers expect lower performance from women and therefore mothers are less likely to be hired, promoted, and fairly paid in the workplace.[27]

Mothers' starting salaries are statistically 7.9 percent lower than otherwise equal childless women and 8.6 percent lower than fathers. Fathers are actually paid better than men without children, being offered $152,000 as a starting salary over $148,000, respectively.[28] For that reason, when many families had to choose who should step out of the workforce to be the homeschooling teacher or provide childcare for their kids, the woman was primarily the choice martyr.

A McKinsey study found that nearly 2 million women felt pressure to leave the workforce or step back from their careers for their families.[29] Not to mention, any time you take away from work impacts your earning potential. It also puts an unfortunate gap on your résumé and prevents or limits you from providing for yourself or your family in a situation where your partner can no longer work, suddenly passes away, or you experience a divorce.

So if you're someone who feels the need to comment that "No one should raise a child but their mother," I'd ask you to think to yourself whether society puts that same burden on the father. Think about that when you ask women what their childcare plan is when they're about to enter a busy season of work or take on a new professional project.

Most of us feel guilty enough knowing we'll be away from our child while we're working, but there is added shame from external sources when we're made to feel like the only responsible party to care for a child.

My husband and I are equal partners, which means that he takes on the same amount of emotional and physical labor that I do as a parent. No woman should have to do it all alone if they're in a partnership—romantic or otherwise.

So, please, stop normalizing this narrative.

Stop saying, "Who is watching your kid?" when women are doing things solo. It might be shocking for some of you to hear this, but a woman can exist as an individual outside of being a mother. Stop asking women, "Is he going to be okay?" when they tell you their partner is watching their child. Men shouldn't be held to a low standard when they are equally responsible for the well-being of their own children. Stop referring to male parents as babysitters! Full stop.

Women should not always be the ones who have to take on the additional mental burden of organizing and managing their family's every waking second. Instead, worrying about laundry, cooking, cleaning, and childcare should fall on both partners.

If you are a mother, make sure you prioritize your career and your earning potential in the same way your partner does. You need to protect yourself and your financial situation just as much as they do.

BUT HOW DO YOU PREPARE FOR THESE TYPES OF EMERGENCIES?

What I've learned from most of my interactions that involve money is that no one likes a surprise—unless that surprise is the lottery, of course. Instead, most of us would rather prepare for any possible mishap that could impact our financial journey.

When life unexpectedly hands you a significant challenge, it can feel like the walls are caving in. But, before you panic, it's essential to acknowledge that there is always time to get organized and create a plan that works for you.

The most common question I get from readers is how to prepare for these moments. For example, how do I financially prepare for a child? How do I speak to my parents or in-laws about their retirement plans? And, also, what should you do when you already know you will be financially responsible for taking care of your parents as they age?

Whether it's an unplanned pregnancy, an unexpected death, or an unforgettable divorce, each of these situations requires careful consideration of the financial implications. So how can you prepare yourself and—if it's too late—what are the next steps?

First things first: You already know that having an emergency fund can protect you in some sense of the word. It's there for the financial difficulties we can't predict. But even better than an emergency fund is having a plan—and knowing when to put it into action.

Second, there are a few very essential things to take care of when it comes to family changes, life changes, or preparing for the most uncomfortable change of them all—death.

Let's consider death more seriously, though. *Seriously* is the keyword. That means that if you're doing that thing we all do when we're reading—when we start to fantasize about something concerning what we're reading, but we forget to digest what we're reading—now is your reminder to come back to focusing on these words first.

We hate to talk about death, yet it's inevitable. We, as a society, try to delay death, deny death, cheat death, and do anything we can to avoid the idea of this contract that we sign when we're born, saying we'll live and then we'll die. Morbid? Perhaps. But, as much as I love a good vampire series, probably because it provides us with the visual of that eternal youth we all desire, I know that it's not the reality.

At one point or another, we all must confront death, whether it is a family member or a friend's unexpected passing, a miscarriage, or a long-term illness finally reaching its conclusion. Rather than pretending that things will all work out, we need to acknowledge that death is something we should talk about more openly. The end of life doesn't have to be taboo or morbid. Just like money, it exists, and it's crucial to discuss. Talking about death doesn't mean it will arrive any sooner. It just means that you'll be more ready for the time when it finally does.

When Cameron Huddleston, author of *Mom and Dad, We Need to Talk: How to Have Essential Conversations with Your Parents About Their Finances,* found out that her mother was experiencing significant health issues that would prevent her from being able to manage her finances and more important, herself, she had to step up.

Cameron was only thirty-five with two young children when her sixty-five-year-old mother was suddenly diagnosed with Alzheimer's. Until this point, the mother and daughter duo hadn't had many conversations about money or what the future might look like should something significant happen.

So as soon as things started to change, Cameron became aware that she would be responsible for her mother's healthcare decisions and finances.

The top three considerations for any financial emergency that involves family are:

1. Engaging in these difficult conversations
2. Setting up an estate plan and a will
3. Transitioning your finances during a difficult time

"If you don't have a plan for your parent's finances or your own, you're going to run out of money—or you're going to run out of money faster than you thought," says Cameron. So talking to your parents or loved ones about these issues should be a priority.

Talking about money may be awkward and uncomfortable for anyone, especially aging parents, when the conversation is initiated by an adult child. Your parents are the ones used to giving you advice, so a role reversal might be difficult for them to handle.

A gentle reminder, though: You don't want to wait for any financial or healthcare emergency to force you into a conversation about money. At that point, it will be too late. So, instead, have these conversations early and often.

THREE WAYS TO TALK ABOUT MONEY WITH A LOVED ONE:

Cameron says that the best way to ask someone about their financial plan is to ask them for advice. Although that may sound counterintuitive, this way, you can get clues without directly confronting someone on a sensitive topic.

1. USE A STORY OR A CAUTIONARY TALE FROM A "FRIEND OF A FRIEND."

My friend Leah's mother passed away without a will. I can't imagine having that added stress on top of losing a parent. What do you think?

2. USE ONE OF YOUR LIFE CHANGES TO ASK FOR PERSPECTIVE.

Because we just had our first baby, we're thinking about purchasing term life insurance to ensure they would be okay financially if anything were to happen to us. What do you think, and do you have life insurance?

3. SHARE A WHAT-IF SCENARIO.

I want to let you know that you can find my estate plan here if anything should happen to me. If you were to pass away or suddenly be in a coma, do you have a similar plan? And, if so, where would I find those documents?

Talking about money and what your parents may have planned for their future involves a series of conversations. Cameron says you'll want to find out where their documents are, how they pay their bills, what banks they use, and more. For that reason, you want to take it slow and avoid pushing too hard and fast at the start.

"If they're reluctant the first time you talk, don't give up," says Cameron. "Try talking to them through someone else they trust and look to for guidance." In any emergency, you will deal with a heavy flurry of emotions. So the more you take care of before emergencies come up, the better.

"Sorting out as much as you can in advance will make those difficult situations a lot easier," says Cameron. Especially so when you can divide and conquer those roles and conversations with your siblings or cousins.

CULTURAL EXPECTATIONS WHEN IT COMES TO TAKING CARE OF LOVED ONES

For some, the responsibility of taking care of your parents' or another loved one's financial situation is less of a priority. For others, it is more of an expectation. Depending on your upbringing or culture, it may be glaringly apparent that you will be in charge of your parents' retirement plan. More specifically, you will be your parents' retirement plan.

Connie Conpoint, a twenty-nine year-old Chinese

American tech worker who dreams of financial independence to retire early (FIRE), is on track to do just that at only thirty-five years old. But she is also doing her part to make sure her parents can achieve the same kind of financial freedom.

When Connie was a kid, a large part of her upbringing revolved around supporting family members. "It is something that is almost ingrained in Asian kids growing up—especially for those of us who are second-generation immigrants, where our parents sacrificed a lot, simply moving to the United States."

Connie's parents were always transparent when speaking about money, worries, and fears about the future.

"I always knew that money was important," says Connie, who admits that she has never bought into the idea that money can't buy happiness. "For a lot of people who struggle, the root is financial instability."

To her, although money can't buy you success, it can buy you the foundations to pursue the things that matter more than money: things like peace of mind, reassurance, and even professional risk.

Before she started her financial journey, she hadn't had a conversation with her parents about their retirement plans. Once she finally did, they told her that all they want for Connie is for her to feel happy. They told her they don't need her money and that she shouldn't worry.

But, as she said, taking care of loved ones is ingrained in her culture, and although it may not be an expectation, she still feels the need to prepare.

Each payday, Connie puts aside a portion of her earnings to plan for her parents' retirement. Then, she sets the money aside, pretends it's gone and doesn't include the fund in her savings rate or personal net worth.

Although this may seem like a financial burden to some, Connie is exceptionally grateful for all her parents' sacrifices. So providing for them down the line doesn't seem as big a deal as it may to others.

"Money is highly personal," says Connie. "When you add in family dynamics, it becomes ten times more personal." For that reason, she doesn't necessarily think that this is a budget line that makes sense for everyone. But if you feel that you will need to support your parents in their retirement, it is never a bad idea to have the conversation.

If you've become aware that you are the one responsible for your loved ones' retirement plan, or if you're dealing with an unplanned baby, a surprise divorce, or a healthcare scare, there are a few things you can do. One of these is to set up your will or estate plan or have your loved ones do the same.

When it comes to talking about death, those conversations rank right up there with *Things I never want to do on a Friday night*. But all joking aside, that doesn't mean we should put these conversations to the side and pretend the issue doesn't exist.

My friends, who are mostly nurses, never gave me the chance to feel uncomfortable talking about death. Within one month of starting her first job at a hospital, my friend Alessandra came to my house to get ready for a girls' night. Somewhere between doing our hair and applying way too much bronzer, she point-blank asked me if I could sign a legal document saying I would be her personal healthcare decision maker.

"What the hell is that?" I asked as a naive and slightly tipsy twenty-one-year-old.

She explained to me that if she ever got into an accident that would cause her to become debilitated or in a permanent coma, she'd want me to be the one to say the doctors could unplug her machines.

"I never want to be a vegetable, and I know you're the only one who would follow through with doing what I want," she said.

I didn't know whether to be offended that she thought I'd be okay with pulling the plug or flattered that she knew I understood. But, as her friend, I wanted to be the one who would follow her wishes, no matter how terrifying and paralyzing it was for me to think about her dying. So I signed the document and, in my early twenties, was suddenly responsible for enacting someone's end-of-life directive.

In a 2021 wills-and-estate-planning study, two out of every three adults still don't have a will, despite the global COVID-19 pandemic.[30] Erin Bury, CEO of Willful, online will-planning software for Canadians, says that we always hope the worst never happens. You never want your home to burn down or your car to stop working suddenly, but we have insurance to guard against these things. So why should safeguarding our assets and providing a plan for those we leave behind be any different?

"We tend to put off these mortality-related documents because they are just a bit uncomfortable to deal with," says Erin. But what's important to recognize is that a will is not for you—it's for the people you leave behind. "Much like life insurance, you do not benefit from that policy," says Erin. "Only your family will, and by having these documents, you can remove the uncertainty."

I asked her how she would convince someone to change their mind about creating a will if they were on the fence or felt it wasn't a necessity, and she wrapped up the answer beautifully with a cherry on top:

"You spend your entire life trying to grow your assets and grow your wealth. A will is the easiest way to ensure that your wealth is passed down efficiently. You can't say you want to provide for your family and in the same breath say that you don't need a will."

In the past, creating a will was complicated, expensive, and required going to a lawyer's office to have your paperwork notarized. Nowadays, if you have a relatively simple life and not many assets, you can take care of the entire process from your own home in less than an hour.

Gone are the days of making excuses for not taking care of a financial task because it seems overwhelming or complex. Instead, the best thing you can do is choose an online or in-person provider and start the process.

WHAT DO YOU NEED WHEN COMPLETING YOUR ESTATE PLAN OR WILL?

► Birth, death, marriage, and divorce certificates
► Deeds or mortgage documents
► Bank account information
► Investment portfolio and brokerage information
► Insurance policies and numbers
► Funeral or celebration-of-life information

YOU WILL NEED TO SELECT:

► An executor: The person responsible for carrying out your will and requests
► A power of attorney: The person responsible for all your financial assets
► A personal directive: The person to make decisions on your behalf if you are unable to do so yourself
► A legal guardian: The person(s) responsible for taking care of your children
► Beneficiaries: How you will split your estate and to whom your assets will go

Not every milestone in life is planned or welcomed with open arms. Illness and death of a loved one are difficult enough as it is. So the added fact that it can set you back financially is tough. The last thing we want is to think about these tragedies. But planning for these unknowns is perhaps the most critical step.

Financially, any family milestone can be expensive. But there are a few things you can do to move forward with fewer worries. Take note of what these unexpected expenses could be. If you are in a relationship, if you have elderly parents, or become pregnant, it's never too early to plan.

Although it may seem unnecessary, saving for these future events can be the best financial habit to build. Strangely enough, although I had never intended on getting pregnant, I had started a small savings account for my future family needs. When I got the positive pregnancy test, the account already had $500 in it, which was enough to feel like I had some control over my situation.

There is nothing wrong with saving for a wedding or a child (even if you're single), or a health concern (that may not yet exist). In the event you no longer want or desire those things, suddenly you have saved up enough money to take a luxurious trip to Europe.

My husband once told me that the best way to get through to someone when you want them to take a topic more seriously—like money or death—is to relate the concept to childhood or the end of their life. If they aren't close to either of those events, if they're somewhere in the middle of their life cycle, your best bet is to focus on the people closest to them.

So let me ask you: If you vanished off the face of the earth tomorrow and were to think about all the people in your life, would they be okay financially? Would they need time off work? Would they be able to support themselves and the other people in their lives without you in theirs?

These questions and answers are the only ways to get us thinking that having a plan isn't about us. Instead, it's about the people in our lives who need us—and that may be more people than we realize.

Since we've been spending so much energy talking about our parents and how we can support them, what can we do as parents to support our children? Particularly when we don't want to be dependent on them in our retirement or illness.

WHAT ABOUT THE KIDS?

The day I became a parent in 2018, money and saving more became the common themes that would replay in my head at the end of each day. Whether it was finding ways to save for a college education or wondering how much we'd spend on extracurricular activities when she was older, I spent many hours hoping we could afford to give our daughter everything she would need.

I'm not alone in this worry. Every parent deals with some anxiety, and mine just so happened to center around money. For that reason, we've always found ways to save money, stay on top of our financial security, and look for ways to create a stable environment for our family.

First of all, saving money for your children isn't as straight-forward as it is when it comes to most other financial goals. For one thing, having children costs a lot of money, which means that saving isn't and can't always be our top priority.

I think it needs to be said that it's perfectly okay to prioritize a non-budget-friendly item if it means your child will be taken care of in whatever way you deem essential. Nevertheless, here are five key things we can do to save money as parents.

1. RESEARCHING SALE CYCLES

One of my personal favorite ways to save money on what our daughter needs is by researching sale cycles for clothing and accessories. A sales cycle is a company's routine in selling an item to a customer. From the product's creation to closing the deal, every company has the same goal: selling all the things they produce.

Therefore, at a certain point in the sales cycle, companies are more willing to sell than they were at launch. Now, although it can be hard to guess what size your child might be wearing one year down the road, an accurate estimate can end up saving you a ton of money. We usually do this by looking for items for the following year at the end of each season.

For example, at the end of summer and in the New Year, we'll begin to look for winter and summer clothing for the next time those seasons roll around. Why? Most clothing companies tend to roll out their following line of seasonal-based clothing at these times, which means that there is usually an end-of-season sale. Doing this can also save us money come the birthday and holiday season when we've already pre-bought some of her gifts during the off-season.

2. AVOIDING COMPARISON

Another financial burden of being a parent is the constant comparison with other families with children similar in age or who have already been through this season of life. Whether it's a fancy stroller or designer clothing, it can be hard not to feel that you should be spending more so that your child can keep up with their closest friends.

I used to feel shame and guilt for not buying the brand-name items or buying a more conservatively priced item that was the best fit for our budget. These days, I've changed my tune. If you're wondering how I got over the comparisons and competition between families, it was by reminding myself of the following things:

- ▶ My budget exists for a reason, and it is what keeps us able to afford the current lifestyle that we have crafted and love. If we wanted to live a different lifestyle, we would have to change many things that make us happy, such as flexibility and time together.

- ▶ Every children's item passes the same safety test, which means that, to a certain extent, any extra dollar you spend on an item is to pay for the brand name. It may come with some additional accessories or features that a more affordable and straightforward item in the same category may not have, but if the goal is to keep your child happy and safe, everyone is on the same playing field.

3. SELLING AND ACCEPTING SECONDHAND ITEMS

An easy way to save money as a parent is to elect for secondhand and gently used items. Whether you get these things from a family member, friend, or thrift shop, they are all going to provide you with what you need at that moment. Half the time, these items are equally as good as new ones because they are only used for short periods. Kids grow quickly, making it difficult to justify spending a fortune on clothing, toys, and accessories. I'd much rather take those savings and put them away for her later years when life might become a bit more costly and complicated.

4. PARTICIPATING IN FRUGAL ACTIVITIES

My child is young and, therefore, nearly anything new or outdoors is exciting. Not all kids need fancy or overpriced events and outings to feel loved or happy. Instead, we find our daughter equally excited about a hike in the mountains as she has been about a paid dance class.

5. USE SINKING FUNDS

The last and potentially most essential savings tactic we use as parents is sinking funds. Sinking funds are one way to save money, in which you set aside a small amount each week or month for one goal to be used at a later date. For example, each year, I set up an automatic transfer in which $20 per week goes into a high-interest savings account specifically created for our Christmas fund. By December, I will have over $900 to put toward gifts or decorations.

As a parent, I love sinking funds because they can eliminate the stress of coming up with a significant amount of cash during a time that can feel as if all you do is spend money. Sinking funds can be a great way to save up a child-care fund, vacation fund, birthday fund, or any short-term goal that requires a small amount of money to put away each month.

Ultimately, there are a ton of unique tactics that parents can use to save money. But what I've found is that the best way to keep on top of your financial needs as a family is to regularly check in with your budget, set short- and long-term goals as a team, and make sure that you live within your means. If you have a plan—and a backup plan—money can feel less like a chore and more like a way to get you to the future you hope to achieve.

TAKEAWAYS FROM THIS CHAPTER:

- ▶ Life can come at you fast, but if there is one thing you can always control in some sense, it's the financial aspect of an unplanned emergency. It might not be perfect, but there are options.
- ▶ Talking about money with loved ones is hard but necessary. So it's okay to keep trying, keep asking, and keep opening the doors for communication.
- ▶ If you are a parent of a young child, there are many ways to save money on gear and activities.

9

PUT YOURSELF
AND PAY YOURSELF FIRST
NAVIGATING FINANCIAL ABUSE AND STAYING AFLOAT

WORK IN MY LATE TEENS was just "work" and had no particular meaning. Ultimately, it was just about earning enough
money to pay for silly trips to Tim Hortons, bags filled to
the brim with 5¢ candies, and an obscene amount of clothing from Forever 21.

But in my twenties, things were different. I had just
graduated from university with my communications degree.
So, like anyone who escapes college *mostly* unscathed, I was
fresh on the hunt for any job. Regardless of pay, hours, and
industry, I was eager to get into the working world because
that's what every member of my family had done.

I wanted to put my stamp on the world and start to
build a life that meant something to me. Move into a new

apartment, buy a kitchen table, set up a cute living room that would be the perfect place for my friends and me to hang out on the weekends. I thought that being a career woman was going to change my life for the better. Finally, I would tell people I had a *real-ass* professional job because *real-ass* seemed like the most intelligent way to describe my first full-time career.

So I applied for hundreds of jobs. I spent my entire summer post-graduation tweaking and editing my résumé so that it would stand out. Make my name more prominent, font size 16, let them know I'm bold like that—just twenty-three-year-old things.

And one company bit. It was a school bus transportation company in need of a communications specialist. So suddenly, I—the girl who hadn't washed her car or had an oil change in at least two years—was going to have to convince the manager in my interview that I "love transportation, know all about it, and can change everything wrong with this department and brand."

On the morning of my interview, I walked into the building, portfolio in hand, decked out in professional attire. Two older women who worked there gave me the up-and-down look of *How old is this girl?* or *Is there a field trip today that nobody told us about?*

It stung a little. I could feel the judgment oozing off their bottom lips. But I went forth and snuck into the women's bathroom down the hall. I locked myself in a stall, stood legs wide, arms on my hips, head toward the sky, and practiced a "Hero Pose" that I had learned about in a *fake it till you make it* TED Talk from earlier in the week. It made me feel better about myself, but it didn't take much to boost my confidence back then. So I strolled into the interview room with no fear.

The manager seemed nice. We introduced ourselves, had some casual conversation, and he made some lame jokes that I pretended to enjoy—something I'm used to as a young woman—and we got into the meat of the interview.

I nailed every question, didn't skip a beat, and told him I'd be able to handle any challenge. He wasn't shy and told me that the company culture wasn't ideal and that there was more work than staff. But twenty-three-year-old Alyssa didn't know those were red flags back then. All she heard was *exciting challenges* and *co-workers who don't get along.*

I never had a problem working on teams because I had played sports my entire life. "One bad seed can tarnish a game, sure, but there's no way they could tank a whole company," I thought to myself that night. Little did I know, *he* was the bad seed.

Within twenty-four hours, I got the call saying that I was their top choice. The pay would be $42,000 annually, and the hours would be 8:00 a.m. to 4:00 p.m. Monday through Friday. That sounded like a lot of money! That sounded like my dream! So I said yes—no negotiations, no questions, no fears.

Like most people who start their first real-world job, my eyes were big, and my dreams were bigger. Until this point in my life, anytime I had a creative idea, I would pursue the idea, and my friends and family would root me on. But in the first few weeks of this new job that finally made me feel like an adult, I quickly realized that there were many more roadblocks in corporations.

One month in, my manager was suddenly not as lovely as I once thought. Instead, he slowly began to start texting me personal messages. Although evening texts from a boss are never appropriate, they started harmlessly. Now I know that any messaging outside of work hours isn't typical— particularly when it has nothing to do with work.

Given that I'd never had a real-world job, though, I had no idea. So in my mind, having a boss who considered me a peer or a friend was *cool* and gave me an edge over my co-workers.

Within a few weeks, though, the messages turned from him casually mentioning taking me on vacation to Mexico to sexual innuendos and personal relationship problems with his ex-wife. I wasn't sure what to do, and because I was still on probation, I felt like I had to lie low and be "nice" by responding. But, on the other hand, I was afraid of what might happen if I said I was uncomfortable. This was the first time I learned that I would never regret taking time off to do what I love, be with who I love, or focus on my mental health. But I would regret prioritizing a job that never prioritized me.

Spoiler alert: Your job should never make you feel that you are unsafe.

Text messages aside, my personal life wasn't exactly seamless, either. I was living in my first rental, paying all of my bills for the first time, and already had enough consumer debt and student loans to paralyze my ability to save up money, let alone quit my only source of income. What did this mean? Well, it turned out that living paycheck to paycheck without an emergency fund was keeping me in an unsafe work environment.

Any event that impacts your financial stability, whether a one-time experience, short-term crisis, or a long-term issue, like my work situation, is a financial emergency. So when I first learned about financial abuse, I realized that's what I was dealing with in my workplace. Perhaps even more important, this was workplace harassment.

Financial abuse is a tactic of exploitation or coercion to control a loved one, partner, or peer's financial stability. You commonly see financial abuse in romantic and working relationships, but it can spread much further than these two spaces.

I've often had followers or friends share stories that are forms of financial abuse—but they don't yet realize that fact. So when I did a call-out for examples on Instagram, questions like "Is it financial abuse when your partner guilts you into sex because he pays for things and buys you things or is that just regular abuse?" began to pour in.

From an ex-fiancé trying to trick a woman into marriage for her credit score, to a friend of mine who became responsible for five-figure indebtedness because her ex-boyfriend put their big-ticket purchases in her name, it can happen to any of us. But a few stories in particular need to be shared.

Jennifer (not her real name) was just twenty-two at the

start of her relationship. She was head over heels in love with her partner at the time, and not a thing in the world could make her believe she was in an abusive relationship. At first, the financial abuse started with small expenses her partner asked her to cover, such as a $2 iTunes music download or a $5 coffee—hello, 2000s.

WHAT DOES FINANCIAL ABUSE LOOK LIKE?

Financial abuse refers to actions by someone, designed to control another person's ability to earn, manage, and maintain their own financial situation. Studies show that financial or economic abuse is a common theme in domestic violence survivors. For example, in one report, "Measuring the Effects of Domestic Violence on Women's Financial Well-Being," all of the 103 survivors reported psychological abuse, 98 percent reported physical assault, and 99 percent (all but one) experienced financial abuse.[31]

Katie Hood, CEO of One Love Foundation, says that financial abuse can take many forms. But, most obviously, it can involve restricting access to the money and capital needed to function in life. "For example, if a partner dictates a weekly or monthly allowance that is inadequate to cover needs, or overly scrutinizes every expense, berating you for overspending."

One Love was founded in honor of Yeardley Love, a twenty-two-year-old college student whose life was tragically cut short when her ex-boyfriend killed her. Her family learned during the trial that her death could have been prevented had they recognized the signs of an abusive relationship. Since then, the One Love Foundation has educated more than 1.5 million young people through educational workshops, both in-person and online, by teaching them the signs of unhealthy and healthy relationship behaviors.

Katie says that financially abusive partners might cut off access to bank accounts or hide funds, or they may steal funds from you. They may also excessively spend, leaving their partners feeling vulnerable and anxious. Ultimately, every form of financial abuse begins and ends with an abuser's desire to have control and power in a relationship.

"Why would you break up with someone over $5 or $10?" she would think to herself. But eventually, it extended to more significant purchases. The escalation was so incredibly gradual that she had built up denial as a coping mechanism by the time it became apparent. The pair were married, owned a home together, and shared all their finances.

When they first got together, the two earned the same salary. However, ten years in, Jennifer's partner was earning nearly double what she did. But he still made it clear that she would cover 50 percent of shared expenses and 100 percent of costs that *he* deemed personal, such as the dog the two bought together. Jennifer would cover nearly 80 percent of utilities, groceries, property taxes, and insurance—whereas her husband would continually buy fun stuff and come up short for their essential bills.

At this point, she put all the household bills on her line of credit to get by, while he made sure to put any ownership papers in his name and leave the debt to Jennifer. In the end, she could not continue to save for retirement. The last straw was when Jennifer found out her husband was having an affair and the amount of money he spent on the other woman. So she made a plan to leave.

Jennifer's parents lived across the country, so she relied very heavily on an aunt and uncle who lived nearby. "On average, it takes someone several attempts before they permanently leave a domestic abuse situation," says Jennifer. "It took me two, so I think I am lucky."

One of her most significant lightbulb moments (among many) was the week after they decided to separate. She was driving her poorly maintained vehicle and nearly got into a fatal collision.

"At the time, my husband was driving a brand-new, fully loaded truck that he *needed* to haul his other toys around," she says. "But the true ironic nail in the coffin was that he is a licensed mechanic. He knew exactly how unsafe my vehicle was, even more so than I did."

This experience entirely erased any hint of a doubt Jennifer had about leaving. Had she died in the accident, her ex-partner would have received full ownership of their home, paid off by insurance, and access to her pension.

"In hindsight, I still wonder about that moment because it would have solved a lot of problems for him versus the time and cost of a divorce."

Jennifer says that the first step for her was talking to someone, a family doctor who was able to refer her to some organizations that could help. Her greatest advice for anyone else in a similar situation is to start stashing any little amount of money you can for yourself and your safety.

"It is not a betrayal to do this," says Jennifer. "It is a way to protect yourself."

The second you feel your partner is using money as a method of control, you can do a few important things to protect yourself or a loved one going through a similar situation.

THREE STEPS TO REMOVE YOURSELF OR A LOVED ONE FROM AN ABUSIVE SITUATION

1. KNOW WHAT A HEALTHY RELATIONSHIP DYNAMIC IS.

It can be difficult to leave an abusive relationship if you are unaware of what these situations can look like. Katie says a healthy dynamic around finances in a relationship is when partners can listen to each other and talk through finances, make decisions together and collaboratively agree to disagree, and enable each other to make independent decisions.

2. UNDERSTAND THE DANGERS OF FINANCIAL ABUSE.

"Because financial abuse doesn't happen on its own—it's commonly linked to other forms of emotional abuse—and because during a breakup is the most dangerous time in an abusive relationship, it's important not to just push for a breakup but to be prepared," says Katie.

3. HELP THEIR EXIT WITH A PLETHORA OF RESOURCES ON HAND.

An essential part of exiting an abusive relationship is safety planning. Katie says that if you have the resources—cash, housing, transportation—to support a friend leaving a financially abusive relationship, that is another way to help. Financial abuse is a common reason for homelessness when a person leaves an abusive relationship, so financial support as someone gets back on their feet can significantly help.

Relationships and careers are sometimes challenging to navigate, and money can only make those experiences that much more overwhelming. Whether you are dealing with financial abuse in a relationship, at work, or in your family, the key is to learn how to set up a plan so you can manage various unplanned expenses and give yourself options.

When asking my readers to share some of their juiciest money secrets, one admitted that before she married her partner, she gave her parents $10,000 to safely stow away in case she ever went through a divorce or wanted plastic surgery. I laughed as I read the reply, but, in reality, my wheels were turning. I thought it was brilliant! I told my husband, and he felt the same way. "What an amazing idea," he said. We are both on the same page about separate emergency funds.

To us, there is nothing wrong with protecting yourself and your future—especially if you have experienced a traumatic past or like to have a sense of security in knowing that if anything ever went wrong, you'd be okay. I've said it once, and I'll say it a thousand more times: To achieve financial equity in a relationship, you cannot use money as a weapon. Contributing more financially does not mean that you get to contribute less to the relationship overall. Money is not the *only* way you provide support to your family. It is *one* of the ways you provide support to your family.

"As finances can be a source of conflict in many relationships, establishing early on how you and your partner talk about finances and make decisions together is another important step," says Katie. "You may decide to create separate bank accounts in addition to a shared account if that works better for you—because more than half of all people who escape financially abusive relationships do not have their own."

The essence of a personal emergency fund is something we can't always explain in words but it's something we can feel. If all you need is assurance that you have options, money is one of the most powerful tools to accomplish that.

Finding out that you are a victim of financial abuse, or a loved one is, can be unsettling. But the important takeaway from this experience should be to know that there are options. For example, you are providing yourself with a safety net or emergency fund to prevent the fear of having nowhere to go from setting in and having a support system that can help you when you can't help yourself. Because there is nothing wrong with asking for help.

"You are not alone," says Katie. "Financial abuse is very common." For example, she says that nearly 70 percent of Millennial women have experienced financial abuse by a romantic partner. Her best advice is to reach out to resources that can help and begin planning the action you will take.

WOMEN'S RESOURCES:

- ▶ Visit the One Love Foundation at www.joinonelove.org for resources, tips, and ways to help others.
- ▶ Phone the Office on Women's Health (800-994-9662) or visit womenshealth.gov.
- ▶ Visit www.womenslaw.org for legal information.

Experiencing trauma of any kind can result in many years of work to gain coping mechanisms and tools to rebuild a healthy relationship—or escape a bad one. Money is no different.

At times, financial abuse can cause you to feel like you have a scarcity mindset, in which you feel the need to spend money as soon as you can before it's gone again. Or that you need to save every dollar you earn because it may be taken away too soon. Speaking to a financial therapist (a mental health professional who focuses on your relationship with money) can allow you to create new habits that build a healthy outlook on life and money.

EVEN IF YOU HAVE A "PERFECT" RELATIONSHIP, YOU SHOULD STILL PROTECT YOURSELF

Money in any relationship is never easy, and you never know what might happen ten years from now. For that reason, it's important for you to have good and healthy conversations about money in your relationships. Equality in a relationship that includes a financial partnership (or any partnership) is essential. When two people come together to make money moves, financial obligations become more fun (I swear) and less overwhelming. You can focus on the interests and goals that are important to both of you and use the benefits of an additional income to accomplish those goals in half the time.

Many people who openly discuss their incomes online forget to mention that their financial successes wouldn't be possible if it weren't for their partner. Whether they earn a second income or not—you are at an advantage in ways that others are not. So those of you feeling inadequate because you're not where you want to be and struggle to understand how others your age are already there—don't. If you don't have the privilege of a relationship, your financial game might take a little bit more finessing than others.

If you are in a relationship and feel you don't have a significant other who is on the same page as you financially, it's important to communicate those concerns. Relationships and money are primarily tricky for this reason. Things change quickly, and the discussion about what to do with your money is constant. Talking about it once and hoping that everything will work out is not going to end well. Regular financial conversations with your significant other are meaningful, whether you want to have them or not.

A monthly money date night is a great place to start engaging in these conversations. You need to get to know their financial expectations and set new ones as a team. Everyone grew up in a unique household. No one family is the same, which means that every family manages their money differently. You might have grown up financially sound, whereas your partner might not have had that much security. Their parents might not have had open money conversations, and your parents might have had them early on and often.

Therefore, it's always a good idea to get to know your partner's financial expectations. What do they expect if you were to buy a home together? What about having a child together? Even celebrating a wedding together? The list goes on and on. Get on the same page and talk about your future. It might have everything or nothing to do with money, but you'll never know until you have these discussions.

Equality in a relationship matters. Having equality in your relationship means that both parties contribute equally to every aspect of their relationship. That means that both partners take on household responsibilities, both partners focus on childcare, and both partners provide financially (if they can). The best way to find that equal playing field in your household is to have an open conversation about what equality looks like to you.

Without equality, one partner will likely live in fear. Financially, that means not knowing how they'd support themselves if you took away their access to money. You can determine whether or not you have equality in your relationship by asking some simple questions.

- ▶ Do you make big decisions as a team?
- ▶ Do you feel that one of you takes on significantly more responsibility for managing the household by organizing and making more decisions?
- ▶ Do you feel emotionally exhausted from doing household labor that you and your partner could divide and conquer?

If you answered yes to any of these questions, it might be a great time to re-evaluate how you manage equality in your relationship. Having conversations about money is never easy. But avoiding them can lead to even more difficulty in the long term. The sooner you put yourself in a place that makes tough conversations comfortable, the better off you'll be. You see, like anything else that we learn, talking about money is a muscle. So you have to continually train to strengthen your conversations.

If you are thinking about talking money in your

relationship for the first time or with someone who doesn't exactly love the idea of money, you can do a few things to create an atmosphere that feels and is safe and judgment-free. But first you need to set the mood—in whatever way that means to you. So whether it's dinner at a steakhouse or ordering greasy burgers to go, whatever will make you feel at ease as you navigate money as a team is essential.

Once you're comfortable, it's time to set some ground rules. You can think of it as finding your safe word. So when someone feels anxious or unsafe or as if they're not ready to take the next step, you can stop, do some reflecting, and then come back to the conversation later. Agree in advance on how you'll talk to each other about money and what your acceptable language will be. Like no name-calling or saying, "I'm disappointed in you."

Once you're ready to start, some things that are good to chat about before getting into the depth of the numbers and the budget are your personal relationships with money. Talk about your money story and your upbringing, share some small money mistakes that you've made, reveal what stresses you out about money, and share some ways your partner can help you reduce those worries. Then, when you feel that you have a good grasp of what each other needs in this conversation, you can get to know each other's real spending habits and lay out what you think your financial relationship will be like in the future.

Perhaps one of the most significant financial emergencies we can face is avoiding talking about money with the person we share our lives with. My advice for that is to avoid picking your battles. Instead, pick your poison. What I mean is that you need to work together to find out sore spots that tend to spark your financial tiffs. For example, whenever I saw that my husband bought lunch instead of eating his homemade one, it upset me. We spoke about it, but nothing changed. So I had to remind myself that those lunches were his choice, not mine. There was nothing unhealthy about them, he wasn't spending our savings, and he wasn't harming anyone—especially not me. So I let it go. Acknowledging the things that make us upset—and finding out the why and how we can control those feelings—is incredibly important for money and relationships.

TAKEAWAYS FROM THIS CHAPTER:

▶ Financial abuse can come from platonic relationships, employers, and family members, and it is prevalent in domestic abuse situations.

▶ If you feel you or someone you love is in danger, you should seek help at 800-994-9662 or visit www.womenslaw.org.

▶ Relationships and careers are sometimes challenging to navigate, and money can only make those experiences that much more overwhelming. Even though it might seem like you have nothing to worry about and are in a strong relationship, you still need to prepare by having an emergency fund for you and you alone.

10
SURVIVING AND RECOVERING FROM LOWS

DETERMINE WHETHER DEBT CONSOLIDATION OR BANKRUPTCY IS FOR YOU

LIFE AND ITS MANY EVENTS make you fall under the spell of obligation. You feel as though you have no choice but to buy birthday gifts, Christmas presents, attend gatherings, have wine with dinner, go for frozen yogurt with an old pal, and, well, I could make this entire chapter a list if you wanted me to. But you don't. An obligation is an easy scapegoat for the mass amounts of consumer debt I once faced. I constantly felt I was letting someone down if I didn't follow through on a plan or pay for a $50 cab ride, even though they only bought me a $6 drink.

In university, I wanted to go out as much as possible. It was like an obsession. I didn't want to miss out, I wanted to build memories, and I wanted to spend my early twenties being just that, a twenty-year-old. So when my friends told me they couldn't do anything that night because they had no money, I felt obligated to be their hero. "I don't have any money in my checking account, but I need cash. That must be what this cash advance option is on my credit card. Gosh, golly, these banks sure think of everything," I'd say as I strolled to the bar and ordered four vodka slimes for my girlfriends and me.

It continued no matter what stage of life I entered. For example, I thought peer pressure was terrible in college, but I was about to find out that it was even worse in the service industry. You work a six-hour shift, cash out with your $150 in tips, hang out with your co-workers, and wake up the following day with $35 left over for rent. The feeling that you will ruin your working relationships if you don't stay for a couple of drinks and dinner never goes away. You live paycheck to paycheck over an obligation to match your lifestyle to those closest to you.

When I first leapt into the world of personal finance, I experienced a period of shock that was impossible to escape. Suddenly, the only things I thought about were my debt and my future. Both of which were things I used to happily ignore because I was young enough to tell myself that's a later-me problem. But I quickly realized that I had already passed the age when I should have stopped ignoring my financial situation. I was almost twenty-five, and I had amassed $15,000 in consumer debt across two credit cards, on top of my nearly $7,000 of student loans (which isn't much compared to the six-figure student loans that most American college grads face).

The day after my then-boyfriend, now-husband proposed to me, the panic of "How on earth am I supposed to pay for a wedding?" set in. At that point in my life, I was back in college pursuing a business degree after escaping my toxic work environment  and had no idea what I wanted to do in life. But as soon as we got home from our vacation, I began to apply for jobs. Somehow, one company took a chance on me. It was a not-for-profit debt consolidation organization, and they needed someone for their marketing and communications team, and I scored the job.

The irony and imposter syndrome were not lost on me, that a girl with five figures of debt and no interest in money had snuck her way into the office that first day. But when I sat in on my initial training with a credit counselor helping a single mother of two to organize her finances and debt, I immediately knew I was meant to be there.

Why? Because I was that woman, just five years younger. I had just gotten my wisdom teeth out and for the first time, I couldn't even afford to buy gauze to help with the bleeding. For the first time, I had to dip into my overdraft. For the first time, I had a massive realization that I was in deep financial trouble.

I had credit card debt, no budget, and no idea how to control my spending. If I kept going down the path I was on, I'd be in this same appointment, asking for help and not knowing where to start. So I went back to my desk and started looking up personal finance blogs. Again, I found a plethora of content—some even from people living in my own city. I felt like I had been blind to the fact that other people *actually* talk about money openly with others after being raised in a world where debt was seen as some shameful stigma that didn't have a place in casual conversation. I felt empowered. Like I could do this. I could repay my debt, and I could become "good" at money. So I wrote my first blog post anonymously and emailed it to myself. It was horrible.

A BLOG ENTRY:

Over the next few months, I'd love it if you would join me in my journey. I want to battle the beefy debt monster and educate myself on ways never to let this happen again. What is the best way to save, the best way to repay, and the best ways to keep your life as normal as possible? Normal. Funny little word.

See you soon, my lovely Bitcoins.

Honestly, I'm just impressed with myself for predicting how big Bitcoin would become back then—or even knowing what that term was. Being anonymous didn't last long. I immediately felt comfortable sharing my financial life with strangers on the internet, which made me feel comfortable sharing my financial life with my friends and family. In addition, it was a relief to let people know why I couldn't spend money rather than making up lies to avoid saying I had too much credit card debt to manage. The shame around money is something that we all feel—and this is particularly true when it comes to asking for help. Or worse, filing for bankruptcy.

But when I realized that the more I talked about money, the easier it became to face my biggest fears, the more ambitious I became and the more motivation I had to pay off my debt. My biggest financial hurdle was my credit card debt and my unhealthy relationship with buying clothing.

DEAR CREDIT CARD,

I remember the first day we met—the mailbox down the street that Friday afternoon. You were so shiny, so bold, and so giving. You told me I could have anything I wanted. You told me there were no consequences and that you just wanted to treat me right. You made me feel like a woman for the first time in my life. We had such great times at the mall, the bar, and even online.

Looking back on it now, I feel so naive. How could I have trusted you?

Our days of impulse buying were just a joke to you, weren't they? How could you not tell me your interest rate would go up if I weren't careful? How could you not tell me that you would hurt my credit score if I didn't keep up with payments? You have so much fine print at the bottom of your bills it's like you tricked me into signing a prenup!

Maybe I should be thanking you, though. You changed me as a person. You made me wiser, stronger, and so much more patient. You taught me that saving for something I want is so much more satisfying than just buying it without any concern. You taught me that emotional spending is a real issue, and it can harm your spending habits.

But now it's time you pay up. I'm sick of doing your dirty work. I'm sick of you telling me those jeans I paid $40 for are now going to cost me $60. I knew you saw the bank behind my back, telling them all of the things we were buying. Well, guess what? It's time you went back to where you belong—the back of my mind.

You see, I don't need you anymore. So I found a new partner: cash. And cash can actually afford all of the things you promised me. Cash knows when I should say no. Cash has heard of something called a budget. Did you hear that? B-U-D-G-E-T. What about living within your means? Have you heard of that? I didn't think so.

I'm so over the lies, the bills, and the reward points I can't even use. You told me I would be an adult when I made this commitment, but you truly treated me like a child. There is nothing I want to do more than take some scissors to you and cause you the same kind of harm you caused me. But I won't.

In all honesty, Credit Card, it's not you. It's me. I couldn't control myself having something so powerful with little to no knowledge of who you really are.

In 2015, I tackled all $15,000 of credit card debt in just ten months by changing every aspect of my life, and it felt amazing. But sometimes, dealing with financial stress doesn't have a fairy-tale ending. For the most part, it's hard to find unbiased, clearheaded advice to follow if you don't have a financial cushion to begin with.

In traditional financial advice, you'll hear that if you just "work harder" and "change your mindset," you can turn your life around. But the reality is, for most of us, debt can be suffocating if you aren't making a livable wage. Using data from 2019, the "State of Working America Wages" report showed that even with recent wage growth, the median wage for Americans was only $19.33 an hour, or $40,000 per year for full-time work[32] before taxes and about $41,900 after taxes in Canada.

To some, earning $3,092 each month might seem like a significant amount of money. But if you're living somewhere with a high cost of living, like New York City, for instance, finding a place to rent for less than $3,000 can be tricky—and that's before you take into consideration any taxes, other bills, or debt repayment. Although it's not always our first choice, sometimes the best option is to give ourselves a fresh start and a new opportunity to rebuild our financial life. To do that, you need to either make a change or ask for help.

Suppose you are in a difficult position financially and are dealing with never-ending collection calls from lenders or are in a cycle of making minimum payments with no end in sight. In that case, some options exist to help you take control and move forward to a better place. The most challenging part is deciding which option is best and makes the most sense.

The first option is to repay the debt on your own—which is what I did. Of course, this won't work for everyone. But if you have a decent salary and can cut back on most of your daily fixed and non-essential expenses, it's definitely possible.

HOW DO I PAY OFF MY DEBT?

To pay off my debt, I wrote down a list of my debts and took the time to call each lender to negotiate a lower interest rate. Second, I redid my budget with many more restrictions and I reduced non-essential spending almost entirely. Lastly, I determined what method of debt repayment made the most sense for my situation.

Two popular methods to repay debt are the snowball and avalanche methods. In a debt snowball method, you make your minimum payments across all outstanding debt and put any excess toward the debt with the smallest balance first. This way, you will be able to cross off one debt at a time and hopefully feel more motivated with each final payment.

Using the debt avalanche method, which I chose, you continue to make all of your monthly minimum payments but put any excess toward the debt with the highest interest rate first. Although the debt with the highest interest rate may take longer to pay back, it can save you time in the long run because interest can be what keeps us in debt—particularly when it comes to credit cards. But remember: If you plan to pay off your debt on your own terms, the terms can be what make or break your experience in its entirety.

HOW TO NEGOTIATE DEBT

Negotiating debt can be difficult if you don't know your rights as a consumer. Debt collectors can only contact you to ask about outstanding payments, to let you know they are adding interest or charging you for any late or overdue payments, and to sue you if you aren't able to repay your debts.

They cannot harass or threaten you, and they cannot charge interest rates above your original agreement. Here is how to speak with a collections agent over the phone:

IF THE DEBT COLLECTOR CALLS YOU . . .

"Please confirm your company name and send your request in writing. Then you can call me back at [a specific hour], as that is a better time for me to speak with you."

This gives you space and time to formulate a plan. You can also confirm the debt by checking your credit report to see what debt is owed.

WHEN YOU CALL A DEBT COLLECTOR . . .

OPTION 1: Ask for a debt settlement using a lump-sum payment.

"I can't pay off the entire debt amount. How much would you accept to settle the debt?

"I can pay $___ to settle the debt if your agency finds this amount acceptable. If acceptable, please send me a letter confirming when I need to make the final payment and confirmation that this debt will be paid in full once payment is received on your end."

OPTION 2: See if they have a monthly payment plan.

"I can't afford to pay this amount. Would we be able to arrange a monthly payment plan instead? If so, please send a letter of confirmation [with the agreed-upon amount]."

OPTION 3: Negotiate a lower interest rate.

"In an attempt to pay this debt down, can your agency offer an interest rate reduction? If so, please provide written confirmation of this adjustment."

If the debt collections agency is not willing to negotiate, it may be worth your while to find a non-profit credit counseling organization to help you work out a deal on your behalf.

If you feel like you're not ready or you can't break the mentality that ignoring your debt is easier than actually tackling it, here are four things you can do to finally put yourself first.

1. FIND A MOTIVATOR.

Rather than stating your why, which we've talked about plenty, find an influencer, expert, or accountability buddy who give you the moral support or general education you need. Sometimes having someone on your side is all you need to keep pushing forward. You need a personal finance mentor and motivator, just as some people need a personal trainer.

2. DISCLOSE YOUR DEBT.

Let's stop being afraid to tell those around us our money woes and our money successes. We should be able to shout it from the rooftops and relieve ourselves of that pressure. Bottling up any stress can lead to a lot of anxiety, depression, and mind-consuming battles that no one should ever have to face alone. So please don't be afraid to look for support. It's all around you.

3. STOP BUYING THINGS THAT DEPRECIATE.

We should indeed be aware of where we are spending our money. Will you be getting a return on your investment? People these days have become comfortable with spending their "future" selves' money. Taking out a loan is money that you might have to work an extra ten years to pay back. And after that additional ten years, that product or item you purchased might be worth less than the interest you paid. So ask yourself, "Is it worth it?"

4. QUIT LIVING LIKE THERE'S NO TOMORROW.

This might sound harsh, but sometimes, living in the moment is a sure way to avoid financial success. Yes, tomorrow isn't guaranteed. Yes, you need to get off your phone and breathe in the good times. But you also need to plan and prepare for your future. Investing for your retirement and your future life with a family, traveling the world—or whatever you have on your bucket list—cannot be done short term. Unfortunately, many people haven't even started a savings account, emergency savings, or retirement because of this mindset! Make the switch.

If you want to make the change, but feel that it's too much to manage on your own, debt consolidation can be a happy medium for anyone with a significant amount of debt who can make their monthly payments without too much difficulty.

Typically, a debt consolidator can help put together a plan that focuses on paying multiple types of debt. They will negotiate with lenders on your behalf and work out a lower interest rate and an all-in-one payment plan.

You can reach out to any not-for-profit organization specializing in these payment plans to get an unbiased opinion and determine whether this makes the most sense for you. Or you can find out what other options exist to repay your debt more simply. The third option is either a Chapter 7 or a Chapter 13 bankruptcy. In Canada, you also have the opportunity to take on a consumer proposal, whereby a licensed insolvency trustee negotiates a settlement, which can include income taxes and certain business debts.

CHAPTER 7 BANKRUPTCY

This is the most common type of bankruptcy and requires a federal court to supervise the sale of your assets. However, some assets, like work-related items, household goods, and vehicles, may be exempt from sale.

The money earned through those sales is put toward your debt, and the court system will eliminate all remaining debts. However, a Chapter 7 bankruptcy will not eliminate student loans, alimony, child support, or taxes.

HOW DOES THIS IMPACT YOUR FINANCIAL LIFE?

Depending on the negotiations in court, you may not have to repay the full amount of your debt, discharging some of the totals.

CHAPTER 13 BANKRUPTCY

This type of bankruptcy allows consumers to keep their assets in exchange for paying their debt (partially or in total).

Typically, the courts will put you on a payment plan that takes three to five years to repay your debts.

Although you can keep all of your assets in a Chapter 13 bankruptcy, this filing will stay listed on your credit report for seven years post-filing.

HOW DOES THIS IMPACT YOUR FINANCIAL LIFE?

Since you get to keep your assets if you file for this type of bankruptcy, the only impact will be the note on your credit report for seven years. You can file for Chapter 13 bankruptcy again within two years of repayment.

For people with six figures of debt, bankruptcy can feel like a massive relief. For Sarah Flowers, this was the case. After being hospitalized without medical insurance and already carrying around consumer debt from her younger days, she had accumulated $111,650 of debt.

"The majority was medical bills (totaling $50,000), and about $20,000 was on credit," says Sarah. She also had small personal loans and a car repossession on her list of debts. "I debated filing for over a year mainly because I was unsure of the process."

But after joining a Facebook group through the non-profit organization Upsolve and reading about other people's experiences, she felt she was ready to move forward. For her, the shame was about debt rather than filing for bankruptcy. Finally, the realization kicked in, and Sarah felt that if corporations could file for bankruptcy regularly, she shouldn't be ashamed of using any available tool.

She recommends this process to anyone struggling financially so long as they understand the consequences in their entirety. "I would advise a friend going through something similar to thoroughly research the process using free consultations with bankruptcy attorneys, reading personal stories, and taking time to weigh the pros and cons." Sarah says that bankruptcy can be a clean slate for some people and has been one of the best decisions she's ever made.

The thing about money, and debt in particular, is that it's hardly ever about the money at all. You can be doing everything right with your money and suddenly take three steps back because you forget how to manage those dollars appropriately. Money is problematic when you don't have it, but it's also problematic when you do. The only way to control the problems that can arise is to learn—and continue to learn.

Beau Humphreys, an insolvency counselor, wasn't always in a good financial position. His gambling addiction almost ruined his life and put him into debt so deep it felt as if there were no way out. But, although it was gambling that put him into debt, he eventually found that the root of his financial struggles was his inability to cope with attention deficit disorder.

After receiving help and going on medication, Beau began to get his addiction under control and finally seek financial assistance. He went through a consumer proposal in Canada and started his journey to helping others walk through their most challenging stage of life, just as he had. For most, he says that we consider bankruptcy and consumer proposals to be worse than death. "It's the hardest thing to talk about until you realize it's your one chance for a fresh start," says Beau.

So how can you *actually* go about filing for bankruptcy or considering this option and whether it's the right choice for you? Beau says there are three key steps:

1. Do an audit of your financial life. Take note of your priorities and acknowledge the importance of asking for help in moments of difficulty.
2. Speak to an insolvency agent, a bankruptcy attorney, or trustee. For no charge, they can provide you with a list of what options exist and are available to you.
3. Make the changes to give yourself the opportunity for a fresh start with your finances, and don't feel shame or guilt for having to file for bankruptcy.

"People try to reduce their expenses, but for most, their expenses are already as low as they can go because the cost of living is so high," says Beau. "Sometimes, you just have to go through something like this."

Beau says he lost a good ten years of his life to his gambling addiction. But he realized that there were more than just bad financial habits at play. "There are many fundamental and systemic things that need to change," says Beau, who acknowledges that it is ingrained in people to pay their debts at all costs from birth. "But we need to amend this concept," he says, "to instead, say, you pay your debts if it doesn't ruin your life."

You are not a bad person for having debt that you needed to put food on the table, protect your health, and provide for your family. You deserve the help you need to finally give yourself the upper hand in your financial life and build enough of a cushion or an emergency fund to prevent these continual cycles of paying the minimum balance with no end in sight. Once you finally pay off your debt, the feeling of relief is undeniable. It's almost as if you can physically feel the weight lift off your shoulders. You have so much room to grow, and now, you finally feel that you can save for your future.

BUT WHAT DO YOU *ACTUALLY* DO ONCE YOU BECOME DEBT FREE?

During debt repayment, I learned a lot about how to save money. I learned how to control my spending, build good credit card behaviors and habits, how to rebuild my credit score, and how to save money so that I wouldn't fall back into old habits once I finally started living that dream life I had always yearned for.

The day I paid off my last credit card bill, my monthly automatic contributions started flowing. I had money going to my vacation fund, retirement fund, emergency fund, and even a rainy-day fund. My life became an endless circle of saving.

Payday became less and less of an *Oh my god, it's finally here* and more of an *Oh right, it's payday*. Things felt great. I was feeling fortunate and knew that so many other people didn't get to feel this way. Therefore, I didn't want to take a single dollar for granted. "Everything must be accounted for," I said with conviction.

But that's when I quickly realized that living with a scarcity mindset is very real and troubling. A scarcity mindset is feeling fear that because you didn't have enough food to eat in the past, once you do have enough food, you need to hoard it all in case food is hard to come by once again. It can be genuinely suffocating.

Once you reach the end of your debt repayment journey, a scarcity mindset is a common reaction. Learning how to manage your money appropriately while still allowing yourself the freedom to live life is exceptionally challenging. Many people save and save and save all their money because they never want to go back into debt. Others spend and spend all their money because they finally have it after not having it for such a long time. I was in the save and save and save category.

After becoming debt free, I was afraid to spend my money.

In the year following my debt freedom, the only money I spent was on my wedding. I saved enough so that I wouldn't have to go into debt for the big day and so that I wouldn't leave that day with any balance owing on my credit cards. It worked. I managed to pay for my wedding in full. I decided to hold off on my honeymoon so that I could save enough to avoid going into debt yet again. It's still working. Before buying anything significant or even purchasing anything small, I save for that item before I buy it.

However, it became more of an addiction for me to save everything I earned rather than to spend it. "Why would I want to spend any money if I could save the money?" I thought. And then I found out that I was pregnant, and my mind started to spiral. Children are expensive. Babies need a lot of stuff. I am not ready to give up my financial freedom. How will we provide for this kid? Can we afford this kid? Will we go into debt? Do you see where I'm going with this? All of a sudden, I panicked and entered a scarcity mindset again. Once I found out I was pregnant, every dollar I earned went into my savings account (except for a splurge on a family vacation).

Then one day, I let myself make what seemed like a harmless purchase, and I couldn't stop. In other words, it was my first glimpse into what happens when you don't learn what sits at the root of your financial difficulties.

I spent over $1,200 within one week after going nearly fifteen months without buying myself anything, and I have no one to blame but myself. Living frugally didn't suddenly turn me into some spending monster who had no self-control. However, I learned that by restricting myself for over a year, I had forgotten what it was like to purchase something for myself as a responsible adult.

So if you're currently paying off debt or are nearing the end of your repayment, here are my best tips for what you can do to avoid being overly restrictive.

YOU'RE NOT A ROBOT.
YOU DON'T HAVE TO RESTRICT YOURSELF FROM EVERYTHING.

Choose one or two of your favorite "fun" parts of life and pencil them into your budget. Buying new clothing and new makeup without a plan is okay. But you could put away $20 a week, and then when you find a sweater you really love, you'll already have a good chunk of savings and the purchase won't put you in a bind.

AVOID SAVING JUST TO SAVE.
I'VE SAID IT (MORE THAN) ONCE, AND I'LL SAY IT AGAIN.

If you don't have a plan for your money, it's not going to end well. By just keeping money sitting stagnant in your checking account, you're setting yourself up for failure. Set a goal, invest the money, or be realistic in the fact that if you don't have a plan, you'll end up blowing that money on something silly.

SELF-LOVE ISN'T JUST ABOUT SPENDING.

Suppose you're truly dedicated to debt repayment or saving for a more substantial financial goal. In that case, it's essential to understand that there are other ways to provide yourself with happiness aside from buying material items. Although clothing and makeup make me happy temporarily, I find that reading blogs, watching YouTube, and baking are even more therapeutic than any online shopping spree. Learn what tools work for you aside from spending money.

Being frugal is tough, but often it's necessary. The only advice I can give to you based on my personal experience is that balance is so important. You're allowed to be frugal and still buy yourself a new bathing suit. You're allowed to be frugal and still pick up a coffee on the way to work. No one can say you're not good at saving just because you spend lavishly in other ways. We have the freedom to live our financial lives however the hell we want to—and that's the way it should be.

TAKEAWAYS FROM THIS CHAPTER:

- ▶ You can pay off your debt without help, but there is no shame in using the options available to you.
- ▶ No one deserves to be in debt for paying essential bills. You are not a bad person, and you are not bad at money.
- ▶ Sometimes giving yourself a fresh start and opting for debt consolidation or bankruptcy is the best decision you can make.

it's okay to have
SMALL PLEASURES

CONCLUSION

IN 2020, MANY THINGS in life shifted for most of us. Experiencing my first pandemic made me realize that life only gets more complicated from here. For you, the life shifts might have been greater than or less than mine. In my early twenties, it was easy to (mostly) float through life. Sure, I had anxiety and responsibilities, but those were problems that only I had to experience.

As you get older, more and more people around you begin to experience tragedy that impacts you in ways you never thought possible. There is no more hiding from your friends' highs and lows. You can't always ignore your family problems. Instead, it would be best if you now managed these situations. Because, suddenly, you are the go-to person who knows how to handle life's obstacles.

Like a *really* cheesy analogy, life comes in waves. This past year I've seen the people I love most escape abusive relationships, navigate divorce, recover from miscarriages, face unemployment, and, honestly, just plain struggle. My own mental health has been up and down and I feel pulled in more directions than I can manage. We've been expected to continue to hit deadlines with all of this weighing on our shoulders in the midst of one blow after another.

It hasn't been fun to manage it all while dealing with political turmoil and a deadly virus. But I want to think that most of us realized that there is more to life than going to our job each day and heading home to sit in front of our television for four hours before falling asleep with chip crumbs on our cheeks.

Money can't take away any of our pain and suffering. It can't love us. It can't listen to our fears and tell us that it's proud of our accomplishments. But what it can do is provide for us in moments when we can't provide for ourselves and provide for others who depend on us. Having money can give us the power to make purchases we want without feeling guilt or shame.

Having the financial means to overcome losing a job you gave everything to or escaping a relationship that put you in danger is a powerful feeling. And emergency funds: Although we can't show them off as we would a designer handbag or a brand-new vehicle, these savings accounts are what fuels that sense of freedom so many of us desire in life.

Whether we realize it or not, we are all a little bit afraid to talk about our finances, and we are scared to admit when we make a mistake with our money. But, as I've said before, I still make money mistakes. For example, last week, I went over my data plan by six gigabytes.

Am I a bit unusual when it comes to money? I mean, sure, a little bit. But my money mindset has allowed me to help people. If I tell people I have debt, they will be unafraid to confront their own financial struggles.

It's incredible that even though there are millions of resources, information, and content out there, people are still ashamed to talk about money. Or admit when they don't know something. Stigmas suck. And I want them to go away. Forever. Please. Could you leave us alone? Sometimes I forget that not everyone is cool to talk about money like my internet friends and me. Even my close friends get embarrassed when I bring it up at every social gathering possible.

For many of us, instead of being open to the possibility of helping others to feel less concerned with where they're at, we want to ensure we don't tarnish our own reputation. I mean, I get it. I do. *But when?* When do we start feeling more comfortable talking about money? If not now, is it Thirty? Forty? Fifty?

At this point, I'm afraid it may never be. So here is your wake-up call: Nothing will change until you make it change. Don't know anything about your finances? Research it. Are you embarrassed to talk about your money? Start small. Reach out to close friends and family.

Avoiding saving for emergencies, investing, retirement,

and expenses is not the way to get ahead. The longer you wait, the farther away your goals get. Homeownership, financial independence, travel? They are a lot easier to accomplish when you have a good grip on your money. Trust me.

The thing about money is that when you don't have it, you fantasize about all the things you'd like to buy. And when you do have it, you fantasize about all the money you could have saved if you'd avoided those non-essential splurges. So, ultimately, we all have regrets when it comes to our money.

I have financial regrets, too. Many of my regrets are from my early twenties when I didn't have a stable income or a reason to spend money as often as I did. From increasing my credit card limit to afford groceries to spending my paychecks before I even had them—most of my financial regrets revolve around irresponsible money habits that I could have easily changed. Since learning to manage my finances and understanding the importance of saving, I realize that those regrets are also lessons. Often, I forget what it felt like to have less, and I don't think that's a good thing. I believe that without those regrets and those mistakes, I'd be much worse off today. So maybe your regrets aren't all bad.

We've all made the same mistakes. When I asked readers about theirs, the top regret was spending too much money and living above their means. The second most common response was moving credit card debt to a line of credit for the lower interest rate but following that decision by racking up your credit card balance again. Although some of those financial regrets can seem highly specific, they're much more common than you think.

Here is a list of some of the responses to my question about financial mistakes:

- ▶ Taking on debt to buy a house
- ▶ Impulse shopping for non-essentials
- ▶ Putting vacations on credit
- ▶ Spending too much and not budgeting before we had a family
- ▶ Not saving any income from first jobs
- ▶ Not enjoying any of your income and saving too much
- ▶ Taking out student loans or attending a private college
- ▶ Spending an inheritance poorly
- ▶ Living above means without realizing and then losing it all
- ▶ Not being involved in the finances in a partnership or marriage
- ▶ Buying a brand-new car, rather than a used vehicle

But the thing is, when you hold on to regret, you hold on to blame that you've put on yourself. Sometimes that feeling of shame can help you change destructive or harmful behaviors in the future. Other times the regret can lead to stress. Either way, you need to understand how the regret makes you feel and learn to move on from those negative thoughts. One way to consider how regrets make you feel is by looking at where the guilt might stem from.

For me, I regret not saving enough money at a younger age because I feel as though I've let my future self and family down. However, I've turned this unproductive feeling into a positive by learning to be grateful for the lessons I've learned, and you can do the same.

STEP 1: Accept that humans make mistakes, and, yes, unfortunately, you're just as human as the rest of us.

STEP 2: How does regret harm your mindset today? Please write it down, speak to a professional, and be aware of the negative self-talk.

STEP 3: Forgive yourself.

STEP 4: Focus on the positives.

So you bought a new car instead of a used one. Does that mean you made the wrong choice? Perhaps your new vehicle will be with you for a long time and doesn't cause you stress because you don't need to do as much maintenance on it. So you used to do a lot of spending and impulse shopping when you were younger. Do you still?

Humans change and grow with time. As you get older and more responsible with your money—I'm assuming you're already on the path to accomplishing that, considering you're reading this book—those good money decisions become your new habits. You are more conscious of your spending, more intentional with your budget, and have more realistic financial goals. You cannot change the regret, but you can learn from it.

I'm not a therapist or a certified financial planner, but I am a regular human being who often makes mistakes with her money and tends to overspend without thinking about the consequences. And if there is one thing I've learned in the past ten years, it's that each year I get a little bit better, and those mistakes happen a little bit less often. I hope you can say the same, too! If not, I hope you feel a tiny bit better knowing you're not the only one who has financial regret. You're the furthest from being alone as you've ever been.

To close out this book, I want you to feel that you're walking away with a clear idea of what you need to do financially. But I also want you to get excited about all of the small changes you can make that will make money more fun, less intimidating, and more exciting.

Too many of us have shied away from the conversations about finance because we felt we couldn't find advice or safe spaces to talk about money, salary, goals, and motivations. Not you. Not anymore.

If you feel stuck, want to do more, or are beyond motivated after reading about all the potential issues that you can prepare for, here are thirty-five tricks that will make you say:

I can absolutely do this.

- ▶ Let's start with an obvious one. It would help if you automated your finances. You do enough emotional labor—constantly trying to remember to pay a bill isn't needed.
- ▶ While we're at it, allot yourself some spending money for your bad habits that you keep telling yourself you're going to quit but know you won't.

- Check your credit report. Your score. Regularly. It's good to be aware of your standing and watch for fraudulent activity.
- Got debt? Fill a jar with small numbers on slips of paper. Take one out each week and throw that amount at your debt. Throw it like you've never thrown it before.
- Negotiate, even if you feel cheap. You'll probably never see that furniture salesperson again.
- Update all your online banking passwords. I know you've been putting it off, and so do the hackers.
- While we're at it, remove any saved credit card information from websites. It shouldn't be that easy to spend money.
- Be honest with one trusted person in your life about your money situation.
- Ditch the shorts you think you'll fit into one day. It's for the best.
- Call your credit card company and ask them what they can do for you about interest rates, discounts on annual fees, or, you know, for being a loyal customer.
- Sell or donate all your old things, including clothing.
- And donate more, period. More money, more time, more kindness.
- This is not your father speaking: Take care of your vehicle. That regular oil change might save you from a much higher bill down the road.

- Cancel that membership you never use. Please.
- Read more books about money. Borrow them from your library, rather than buying them.
- Take a financial course to help you better understand your money or investing. Some are free, and some are not. They're all worthwhile.
- Don't park your car where you might get a ticket. We'll never learn, will we?
- Do something you love. I tend to spend less money when I have hobbies to keep me happy and stress free.
- Ask for a raise. You're a total boss, after all.
- Force yourself to look at your bank account regularly. Although I know most of my readers already do this, some people don't. It's better to be aware than guessing when it comes to cash flow. Those money memes joking about being broke are only mildly funny.
- Don't judge others, and you'll automatically feel less judged yourself. It's science.
- Reflect on your last three months of spending and earning. How much did you make, and how much did you spend? It's essential to know.
- Calculate your net worth. If not for anything but to pat yourself on the back for being an incredible person.
- Think about your retirement and what you want.
- Now that you're thinking about it, you should

open a retirement account. Already have one? Increase your monthly contributions.

▶ Prep for tax time. It'll sneak up on you quickly.

▶ Attend a networking event. It never hurts to find new professional friends who could help you move up on the career ladder.

▶ Buy a latte. *Come at me, haters.*

▶ Always use the per-dollar-per-use rule before you buy something. If a pair of shoes will cost you $100, ask yourself if you'll wear them a hundred times.

▶ Think about appreciation. Are you buying something that will benefit you later in life, or will it decrease in value the second you drive it off the lot?

▶ Use Wi-Fi everywhere you go. Ain't no shame in my ask-for-your-internet-password game.

▶ Find ways to encourage yourself and celebrate the little successes that you gain from being more money conscious. Saving $1,000 is a *huge deal*.

▶ Drink less alcohol. Or not. I'm not your momma.

▶ Also, please stop smoking. Now I am your mother.

▶ Care. Your financial future needs you to care.

Like most things in life, it's easy to do the reading and the research, but it's hard to implement those changes into your life. The desire can come from many places, like some of the personal stories you read about throughout this book or an aha moment that made you realize you're not as perfect with your money as you once thought.

We're all doing our best to navigate life and its ups and downs, especially during a time that has put massive amounts of fear at the forefront of our minds and changed how we feel about the future in general.

I'll be the first to admit that I'm not perfect. In the short amount of time I've spent educating myself about finance, my opinions have shifted, and I've grown. I've learned to acknowledge that my perspective isn't the only way to learn and to feel. It's healthy to listen to others and allow yourself to think beyond what you already know. And perhaps now you know that an emergency doesn't have to be as surprising as you once thought.

Remember that life is full of small and memorable moments, but the things we carry with us and that weigh heavily on us are always big, overwhelming, and scary. How you choose to approach those big moments is what matters more than anything else—and having the financial wherewithal to overcome those high highs and low lows is *really* how you win at life and with money.

ACKNOWLEDGMENTS

"WOW. CAN YOU BELIEVE this is *actually* happening?" These were the exact words I spoke aloud to myself the minute I started drafting the proposal for this book. Of course, writing a book in my own words, about my own experiences, is something I've wanted to do since elementary school. But I'm pretty confident that nearly every author would say something similar.

It's a dream to take ideas from your mind—*thoughts that keep you up at night*—and put them on paper. But the reality is that the start-to-finish process of writing a book takes more than just words and characters. It takes a team of people to help you hit every important note, challenge your opinions, check the facts, and confirm that I'm not just an overly paranoid person and that my ideas are an accurate reflection of our universe.

TO MY HUSBAND: While most other partners spend their off time puttering around a golf course or sharing equal *cough* **or less** *cough* parts of parenthood, you're happy to put in double the time and not once complain. It will never be enough to say thank you. I'm beyond fortunate to have a husband who has always told me to pursue my passions and goals without question or doubt.

But for every time I told you "There aren't enough hours in the day," and you responded with "Go and write," I do need to say *thank you*—at least twice. Every conversation we share is, in part, the inspiration behind the many bright sides of this book. So, I'm going to continue to gush over your ability to keep me rational, even though I'm a walking ball of anxiety, until the end of time. You are my person, and I'm beyond grateful life brought us together that first day of college.

TO MY CHILDREN: I hope that you know how much of this book is for you. Each sentence I wrote to provide you with the lessons and knowledge I wish I'd had in my younger days. You are inspiring, motivating, and the reason for my biggest smiles each day.

TO MY PARENTS: Thank you for allowing me to pick your brain over many nights of cards. For allowing me to ask for your perspective and then challenging those ideas with my never-ending list of statistics. For being open to many candid conversations about money, death, climate change, society as a whole, and all the dinner topics that are normally forbidden at family functions. Come to think of it, that's probably why I won every game night, given that my plan all along was to distract you with financial topics.

I feel so fortunate to have two people who care so deeply about self-growth and who could and did provide for me through all of my childhood and for some of my early adult years, too. You gave me the privilege that many other families cannot provide, and I'll never be able to repay you for all that you've done.

TO THE PERSONAL FINANCE COMMUNITY: It's not easy to find a community of people who challenge you and push you to learn about new ideas and concepts as often as ours does. But each of you, without hesitation, was willing to share your expertise and your experiences to make this book more relatable for everyone who should feel safe and welcome when learning about money. So thank you to every single person I interviewed and who reads and follows along with my online content every single day. Your support does not go unnoticed.

TO THE TEAM OF PEOPLE WHO HELPED THIS BOOK COME TO LIFE: To the entire team at Sterling (*present and past*) of Elysia, Kate, Shannon, and more, thank you for taking a chance on me as a writer not once but twice. And thank you for letting me make so many big decisions that I never knew were possible. You are changing my life and many other lives by letting judgment-free money books hit the shelves.

To Erin Lowry, my book coach and a fellow author, who in just two hours gave me the confidence I needed to jump into the process of asking for what I want and writing the things I love to write—thank you.

To my siblings and friends, who kept cheering me on and never let me think that what needs to be done wouldn't get done—thank you.

Lastly, to my mentor and colleague, Romana King, thank you for always believing in my writing talents. The day you took a chance on me was the day I knew I was doing what I was supposed to do, and you have reaffirmed that decision many times with your kind words, heavy edits, and, most of all, advice that has completely changed the way I put words on paper—in the best possible way.

To anyone who reads this book: Thank you. Truly. Thank you for caring about money. Not just for me, but for your future self. Because your future self *really does need you to care*.

NOTES

1. Amanda Dixon, "Survey: Nearly 4 in 10 Americans Would Borrow to Cover a $1K Emergency," Bankrate, January 22, 2020, https://www.bankrate.com/banking/savings/financial-security-january-2020/.
2. "2019 Modern Wealth Index Survey," Charles Schwab Corporation, May 15, 2019, https://www.aboutschwab.com/modernwealth2019.
3. "2019 Modern Wealth Index Survey 2019," Charles Schwab Corporation, May 15, 2019, https://www.aboutschwab.com/modernwealth2019.
4. Amanda Dixon, "Survey: A Growing Percentage of Americans Have No Emergency Savings Whatsoever," Bankrate, July 1, 2019, https://www.bankrate.com/banking/savings/financial-security-june-2019/.
5. "Board of Governors of the Federal Reserve System: Distribution of Household Wealth in the U.S. since 1989," Federal Reserve,

June 21, 2021, https://www.federalreserve.gov/releases/
z1/dataviz/dfa/distribute/chart/#quarter:122;series:Net
percent20worth;demographic:race;population:all;units:
shares;range: 1989.3,2020.1.

6. Paulette Perhach, "A Story of a Fuck Off Fund," The
   Billfold, August 15, 2017, https://www.thebillfold.com/
   2016/01/a-story-of-a-fuck-off-fund/.

7. Loran F. Nordgren, Frenk van Harreveld, and Joop van Pligt,
   "The Restraint Bias: How the Illusion of Self-Restraint Promotes
   Impulsive Behavior," *Psychological Science* 20, no. 12 (2009):
   1523–28, https://doi.org/10.1111/j.1467-9280.2009.02468.x.

8. Eric Young, "Millions of Americans Donate through
   Crowdfunding Sites to Help Others Pay for Medical Bills,"
   press release, February 19, 2020, NORC at the University
   of Chicago, https://www.norc.org/NewsEventsPublications/
   PressReleases/Pages/millions-of-americans-donate-through-
   crowdfunding-sites-to-help-others-pay-for-medical-bills.aspx.

9. "Household Debt Service Payments as a Percent of Disposable
   Personal Income (TDSP)," Federal Reserve Bank of St. Louis,
   August 12, 2021, https://fred.stlouisfed.org/series/TDSP.

10. Chuck Collins, "Updates: Billionaire Wealth, U.S. Job Losses
    and Pandemic Profiteers," Inequality, July 14, 2021, https://
    inequality.org/great-divide/updates-billionaire-pandemic/.

11. Jefferson Bethke, *To Hell with the Hustle: Reclaiming Your
    Life in an Overworked, Overspent, and Overconnected World*
    (Nashville, Tenn.: Nelson Books, 2019).

12. "Social Security Fact Sheet" PDF, Social Security
    Administration, 2017, https://www.ssa.gov/news/press/factsheets/
    colafacts2021.pdf.

13. "Outcomes of Applications for Disability Benefits," *Annual
    Statistical Report on the Social Security Disability Insurance
    Program, 2016*, https://www.ssa.gov/policy/docs/statcomps/
    di_asr/2016/sect04.html.

14. Integrated Benefits Institute, "Health and Productivity Benchmarking 2016 (released November 2017), Short-Term Disability, All Employers." Condition-specific results. https://www.ibiweb.org/wp-content/uploads/2018/01/IHC_Report.pdf.

15. Raymond Kluender, PhD, Neale Mahoney, PhD, Francis Wong, PhD, et al., "Medical Debt in the US, 2009–2020," *JAMA* 326, no. 3 (2021): 250–56, https://jamanetwork.com/journals/jama/article-abstract/2782187.

16. "FastStats—Health Insurance Coverage," Centers for Disease Control and Prevention, June 11, 2021, https://www.cdc.gov/nchs/fastats/health-insurance.htm.

17. "NHE Fact Sheet, 2019," Centers for Medicare and Medicaid Services, https://www.cms.gov/Research-Statistics-Data-and-Systems/Statistics-Trends-and-Reports/NationalHealthExpendData/NHE-Fact-Sheet.

18. Sterling Price, "Average Cost of Health Insurance (2021)," (see p. 122), ValuePenguin, March 05, 2021, https://www.valuepenguin.com/average-cost-of-health-insurance.

19. Christopher Ingraham, "The Staggering Millennial Wealth Deficit, in One Chart," *Washington Post*, December 3, 2019, https://www.washingtonpost.com/business/2019/12/03/precariousness-modern-young-adulthood-one-chart/.

20. Amanda Dixon, "Survey: Nearly 4 in 10 Americans Would Borrow to Cover a $1K Emergency," Bankrate, January 22, 2020, https://www.bankrate.com/banking/savings/financial-security-january-2020/.

21. Glennon Doyle, *Untamed* (New York: Dial Press, 2020).

22. Marty Ahrens and Radhika Maheshwari, "Home Structure Fires," National Fire Protection Association, November 2020, https://www.nfpa.org/News-and-Research/Data-research-and-tools/Building-and-Life-Safety/Home-Structure-Fires.

23. V. Masson-Delmotte, P. Zhai, A. Pirani, et al., *Climate Change 2021: The Physical Science Basis, Contribution of Working Group I to the Sixth Assessment Report of the Intergovernmental Panel*

on Climate Change, Cambridge, Mass.: (Cambridge University Press, in press).

24. Laurel Sutherlin, *Banking on Climate Chaos: Fossil Fuel Finance Report, 2021*, Rainforest Action Network, March 25, 2021, https://www.ran.org/bankingonclimatechaos2021/.

25. Al Shaw, Abrahm Lustgarten, and Jeremy Goldsmith, "New Climate Maps Show a Transformed United States," ProPublica, September 15, 2020, https://projects.propublica.org/climate-migration/.

26. Lustgarten, A., "The Great Climate Migration Has Begun," *The New York Times*, July 23, 2020, https://www.nytimes.com/interactive/2020/07/23/magazine/climate-migration.html.

27. Shelley J. Correll, Stephen Benard, and In Paik, "Getting a Job: Is There a Motherhood Penalty?" *American Journal of Sociology* 112, no. 5 (2007): 1297–1339.

28. Shelley J. Correll, Stephen Benard, and In Paik, "Getting a Job: Is There a Motherhood Penalty?" *American Journal of Sociology* 112, no. 5 (2007): 1297–1339.

29. Sarah Coury, Jess Huang, Ankur Kumar, et al., *Women in the Workplace 2020*, McKinsey & Company, February 18, 2021, https://www.mckinsey.com/featured-insights/diversity-and-inclusion/women-in-the-workplace.

30. Daniel Cobb, "For the First Time, Caring.com's Wills Survey Finds That Younger Adults Are More Likely to Have a Will Than Middle-Aged Adults," Caring, December 2020, https://www.caring.com/caregivers/estate-planning/wills-survey/.

31. Adrienne E. Adams, *Measuring the Effects of Domestic Violence on Women's Financial Well-Being*, Michigan State University Department of Psychology, Issue Brief 2011-5.6, May 17, 2011, https://centerforfinancialsecurity.files.wordpress.com/2015/04/adams2011.pdf.

32. Elise Gould,"State of Working America Wages 2019," Economic Policy Institute, February 20, 2020, https://www.epi.org/publication/swa-wages-2019/.

INDEX

F

V

Vela, Amelia, 78–80

W

Wills and estate planning. *See also*
    Death
  advance medical directives (living
    wills), 153
  reluctance and reasons to
    complete, 154–155
  roles you need to assign, 155
  what's needed for, 155
Women's resources, 174, 179
Work
  income from, 36, 37
  providing options in life, 37

ABOUT THE AUTHOR

ALYSSA DAVIES is a content creator and a published author living in Calgary, Alberta. She is the founder of the two-time award-winning Canadian Personal Finance Blog of the Year, *Mixed Up Money*, with over 40,000 followers across social media. Through her work, she has starred as host of the television show *The Dream Team* and haa been featured in many notable publications, including *The Globe and Mail*, *Market Watch*, and *Real Simple*. Her first book, *The 100 Day Financial Goal Journal*, was published in 2020. Alyssa has been a freelance writer for seven years and enjoys personal finance, homeownership, and mental health stories. When she's not writing, you can find her enjoying some downtime (if that's what any parent calls it) with her two children, playing soccer, or daydreaming about home decor.